HITLER'S BANKER

Jean-François Bouchard

HITLER'S BANKER

Max Milo

Max Milo Editions, Paris, 2023
www.maxmilo.com
ISBN : 978-2-315-01108-7

I hate two kinds of men: those who shirk their duties, those who, afterwards, know everything better than everyone else.

Hjalmar Schacht

INTRODUCTION

What is this old man thinking about as the rickety bus in which he is uncomfortably seated passes through the barbed-wire gates of the Flossenbürg extermination camp in the Upper Palatinate in northeast Bavaria? No doubt to the death that awaits him and the other prisoners in whose company he is closely watched by a dozen or so patient guards. The faces of his prestigious comrades in misfortune betray the same anguish; there is General Hans Oster, who was once Admiral Wilhelm Canaris' deputy at the head of the Abwehr (the Wehrmacht's intelligence and counter-intelligence service), and his right-hand man Theodor Strünck. There is also General Georg Thomas, former head of the war economy and armaments service, General Franz Halder, a high ranking Wehrmacht officer, as well as the Austrian chancellor Kurt von Schuschnigg, who was overthrown during the Anschluss, the annexation of Austria by the Nazis in 1938. Only the presence of Schuschnigg's wife, the aristocratic Countess Czernin, born Vera Fugger von Babenhausen, who carries her 4-year-old daughter in her arms, could have lightened the sinister atmosphere of this convoy to nothingness. But neither the little girl, who was born during her father's long captivity and who has only ever known the sinister world of prisons and internment camps, nor her sweet mother, have the heart to joke.

"We're not getting out of here alive!" the old man bellows in a strangled voice, as the bus passes through the gate under the floodlights of the watchtowers and stops in front of a battalion of soldiers armed with machine guns.

Then the old prisoner is roughly pushed out of the vehicle. The guards lead him towards a greyish building that the darkness of this icy night of February 1945 prevents from distinguishing completely. A poorly lit corridor is walked through at a brisk pace; a door is opened, that of a tiny cell where a straw mattress is rolled up in a corner. The prisoner takes two steps forward. The door is slammed by the guards and the sound of locks being locked echoes for a long time in the building. In the corridor, voices and footsteps are heard moving away.

At last, silence sets in.

The old man, in the half-light of his isolation cell, unfolds the straw mattress and lies down. His hands feel for a blanket and he huddles as best he can under this miserable rag that stinks of filth and death, but the cold is so intense in the heart of the Bavarian winter that he has to do something about it in order to try to keep warm. He closes his eyes. He shivered and could not sleep.

So he probably thinks about the incredible destiny that led him there.

For this old man is not just anyone.

His name is Hjalmar Schacht.

He was the most brilliant financial genius of the 20TH CENTURY.

Hjalmar Schacht saved Germany three times from economic crises that should have led the country to ruin and chaos. Thanks to him, Germany emerged from these deadly crises stronger than it entered them.

But above all, Hjalmar Schacht was the devil's banker.

He was Chancellor Adolf Hitler's big money man. Without Hjalmar Schacht, the satanic Führer of this Third Reich that was to last a thousand years would never have existed. Blinded or seduced by Hitler, he believed that he could control this little mustachioed corporal, this political agitator who harangued the crowds so well, so that he campaigned to bring him to power, then to provide him with the most formidable military arsenal that Germany ever possessed, before realizing his mistake and turning away from him to the point of plotting to overthrow him.

Because when it came to Hitler, Hjalmar Schacht was wrong, he who liked to boast that he was always right and did not fail to make it known.

On this dark night in February 1945, Hjalmar Schacht has been a prisoner of Adolf Hitler for more than six months. In the icy solitude of his isolation cell in the Flossenbürg camp, he sees the end of his story.

And yet! We owe him so much! Future generations would have so much to learn from his life and his work!

He, Hjalmar Schacht, is probably the only financier, the only economist, the only central bank governor, the only finance minister who always knew how to face economic crises and find the right solutions to allow his dear country, Germany, the immortal Germany, to always rise stronger and more powerful. Oh, sure, there are other famous economists who were his contemporaries, Keynes, Marx, Schumpeter, Kondratieff... but he, Hjalmar Schacht, unlike the others, did not remain a theorist. He put his theories into practice, and he succeeded!

Yes, always, invariably, he succeeded!

But he will die here, in Flossenbürg, forgotten by all, and his body will disappear in the inferno of the crematoria, intermingled with those of the Jews, the Communists, the homosexuals and the Gypsies whose attrition is, in this appalling extermination camp, the absurd and revolting industry.

This is undoubtedly the state of mind of the old prisoner, exhausted by the journey, the months of captivity, the cold and the privations.

No.

He is wrong again.

Hjalmar Schacht did not die in this camp in the Upper Palatinate.

He died peacefully many years later, in the comfortable bed of his vast Munich residence, on June 3, 1970. The turbulent destiny of the devil's banker, thanks to whom Adolf Hitler had become the Führer of the Great Reich, which set the world on fire, continued for another twenty-five years after Flossenbürg, with multiple and astonishing adventures: tried as a war criminal, prisoner of the Americans, advisor to kings, princes and dictators, bank founder, miraculously escaping Jewish vengeance... is there anything Hjalmar Schacht didn't do in his tumultuous life?

When death finally caught up with him, he was 93 years old.

On the other hand, there is one point on which he was not mistaken: oblivion. Unlike Keynes, Marx, Schumpeter or Kondratieff, Hjalmar Schacht is not one of the great economists whose theories are studied today on university benches. The fault lies, no doubt, in his unsavory Nazi past.

It's a shame. We could have learned so much from him...

So let's fix this mistake and listen to the voice of Hjalmar Schacht from beyond the grave. In our world of recurring crises, from which few countries manage to escape, Hjalmar Schacht's unwavering determination in the face of the dramatic economic events that shook his country in the first half of the 20th century should have set a precedent among the indecisive and indecisive leaders who have governed and still govern many nations today. This astonishing man has a lot to say and to make understood.

He was able to find miraculous solutions to the unsolvable difficulties he faced, so would it perhaps be enough to pay attention to him to replicate his example?

As for the life of Hjalmar Schacht... it is the authentic and almost unbelievable destiny of a man at the heart of wars, dramas, conspiracies and the backstage of great history, during dramatic decades on which, deliberately or sometimes unwillingly, he has profoundly left his mark.

Much more than a novel!

Chapter 1. The man

I, Hjalmar Schacht, am the greatest financier of the 20th century, and perhaps the greatest in the history of mankind.

I say this with complete objectivity: If I compare my years as head of the German economy with those of my predecessors and successors, if I compare my work with that of all the great leaders, whether in my country or in other great nations of this planet, none of them can boast as many brilliant successes as I have had.

Certainly, I was served by events: to face, in the course of a single lifetime, three economic crises of such critical gravity that the ruin and outright disappearance of my country were at stake, was a unique challenge in history.

So many challenges that I was not allowed to fail.

I have not failed. I have never failed! Failure is not in my vocabulary!

I have often been called arrogant. This is not true. There is no a priori contempt in me towards my contemporaries. But I do not appreciate the insolence of stupidity, the idiocy of ostentation and the absurdity of erroneous reasoning. My whole life has been spent in contact with the world's most powerful and wealthy businessmen. I have often been struck by their superficiality, their ridiculous propensity to display the most extravagant signs of wealth, and their terrifying ignorance in the fundamental fields of economics and finance, which are essential to the running of states. My strict dress and my proverbial sobriety sometimes made people smile. Quite often, in the popular newspapers, I was caricatured as an austere banker in a dark suit, with a hard collar around his neck, steel glasses on his nose, and a condescending look on the face of those I was addressing. Well! I was exactly like that! Feature for feature! The caricaturists were right in every way and I never complained about the flaws they accentuated to the point of distorting my true nature. Because among my qualities, I also know how to recognize talent, even that of the cartoonists who laughed at me.

If I have sometimes seemed contemptuous, it was because I looked with desolation at the abysmal negligence of my opponents. Thus, when Hermann Göring succeeded me as Minister of Economics in 1937, it was immediately clear to me that Germany's prosperity was in danger, and I did not fail to inform Chancellor Hitler of this. As the man responsible for the war economy, the reverend Göring had only been able to take over what I had built up with great difficulty, without really creating anything himself. As for Walther Funk, who took over from me as head of the Reichsbank in 1939, he was nothing but a pale journalist, lacking the slightest capacity for personal initiative and whose only outstanding action, in application of his fierce Nazi convictions, was to obey slavishly Göring, whom he succeeded as Minister of the Economy. With this obese, egocentric, morphine-addicted pervert at the helm of the Reich's mighty economy, and at his side an acolyte whose ability to develop personal theories was of the most minuscule kind, it was certain that my mark, the mark of Hjalmar Schacht, was not about to fade away. And what a contrast in our morals! Their greed knew no bounds, nor did their imbecilic propensity to live like maharajas in obscenely luxurious palaces! Göring was only interested in getting rich, in accumulating property stolen from others. I, for my part, believe that I never tried to profit unduly from the immense power that was entrusted to me. On the contrary: when I joined the Reichsbank as governor in 1933, I simply reduced my emoluments by two thirds, in solidarity with the masses of workers who were suffering from unemployment and for whom my only ambition was to get them back to work. And before that, when I was appointed currency commissioner in 1923, in the midst of the most formidable monetary crisis of our time and at the height of the galloping inflation that was putting most of my fellow citizens out of work, I gave up my entire salary and paid the dedicated secretary I had brought with me personally, out of my own money.

So contemptuous? Perhaps, but only towards the profiteers, the corrupt, the incompetent and the thieves. I, Hjalmar Schacht, believe in the virtue of work, of effort, and of its just reward.

I have often been accused of insensitivity. I would have been, according to my opponents, only a cold and calculating being, as devoid of feelings as a snake whose gaze I often adopted, it seems. Certainly, I am not one of those who feel the need to display their moods in broad daylight. I don't have any moods. My goal is the fate of Germany, my country, my homeland! And I base my attitude on this single objective. There are people who have understood this and who have worked with me efficiently and confidently, because they knew exactly where they stood and what to expect from me.

So, cold and calculating? No; I would say rather rigorous and energetic; a man whose clear thoughts, sense of reality and focus on the goal to be achieved make it easy to understand... for those who know how to understand, of course!

Fortunately, there are some.

With Montagu Norman, my great friend, the Governor of the Bank of England, an intelligent man if ever there was one, we cooperated wonderfully for years, to the point where I can say that without the United Kingdom, Germany could never have become the economic power it was on the eve of the Second World War!

Dear old Montagu, who agreed to become godfather to the son of one of my daughters, is certainly not alone. Many American businessmen came to invest their money in Germany, in the chemical and mechanical industries, in the arms factories, in the banks, on the sole confidence they had in my name. To them, too, Germany is indebted for its newfound power.

But it is above all to me, Hjalmar Schacht, that Germany is to be thanked for having regained its position as one of Europe's leading economic powers. My reputation extended far beyond the circles of business and financial leaders. In political circles, the name Schacht was respected everywhere. Among the famous men for whom I became the universal reference when it came to guiding the economic destiny of our nation was, of course, the old Field Marshal Hindenburg, President of the Republic, who called on me to curb the currency crisis and the galloping inflation. And then, of course, Adolf Hitler, Chancellor of the Reich; but we will come back to that later...

There were many others. I remember with emotion that when he came to power, Franklin Delano Roosevelt, the American president elected in the midst of the great crisis of 1929, asked to see me four times during the trip I made to Washington that year. At the same time as me, the French President of the Council, Henri Poincaré, was also on an official trip to the United States. Roosevelt granted the Frenchman only a protocol audience, while I, the German Hjalmar

Schacht, was received no less than four times in order to give my precious advice on how to get out of this terrible crisis.

Yes, truly, Franklin D. Roosevelt loved me!

This is how the man who became the devil's banker would have expressed himself.

Let us immediately set the record straight. In reality, Franklin Roosevelt could not stand the presence of Hjalmar Schacht, the arrogant, preaching German banker. He hated his pretentious and prideful personality. But as an intelligent and wise man, he recognized that the man's advice was worth its weight in gold...

History remembers Hjalmar Schacht as a brilliant financier who helped bring Adolf Hitler to power and who, thanks to the economic revival and the restoration of prosperity in Germany for which he was responsible, kept him there until the outbreak of the Second World War.

This man's name was Hjalmar Schacht; or rather, according to his full civil status, Hjalmar Horace Greeley Schacht.

It was a curious initiative on the part of the Schacht parents to place their offspring under the patronage of the journalist Horace Greeley, who by the time of their baby's birth on January 22, 1877, had long since left the limelight. In fact, he had only ever shone with a very uncertain light. Horace Greeley was the founder of a newspaper, the *New York Tribune*, which in its time earned the enviable status of the largest daily newspaper in the United States, but it is not for this title that he has remained in history. He is above all the author of a famous phrase: *Go West, Young man! Go West!* which became the foundation of the conquest of the American West. Greeley was also a politician, in conformity with the image that we often have of this congregation; his reversals of jacket were so numerous that they totally misled his potential voters before, disoriented by this disordered strategy of a drunken weathervane, poor Horace Greeley became crazy himself. Indeed, Horace Greeley was one of the most vocal supporters of General Ulysses S. Grant, when he ran for the American presidency in 1868, shortly after the end of the Civil War and the assassination of President Abraham Lincoln. Grant was elected, but then Horace Greeley turned on him, accusing his administration of corruption. Ulysses Grant was then the champion of the Republican Party, one of the two parties that dominated and still dominate the political life of the United States. Greeley founded the new Liberal Party, under whose colors he ran against President Grant in the 1872 presidential election. To everyone's surprise, Horace Greeley was also nominated by the Democratic Party, which he had been deriding in the *New York Tribune* for years. The voters, bewildered by his peculiar political antics and incoherent rhetoric, gave Greeley a real electoral slap in the face, and General Ulysses Grant was re-elected to a seat. Greeley's failing mental health, already affected by the death of his wife just before the election, could not withstand this rout and the unfortunate journalist had to be committed to a sanatorium where he died shortly afterwards, in a straitjacket, even before the results of the election had been announced: the process takes several weeks in the United States

Nothing in this chaotic career appears to have constituted a legacy for Hjalmar Schacht, whose unyielding determination and eyes invariably fixed on the horizon are rather the hallmark.

The choice of Horace Greeley as the posthumous godfather of their second son is, on the other hand, more related to the personality of Hjalmar Schacht's father, whose orthogonal changes of orientation marked the life he imposed on his family. Born a German citizen, he emigrated to the United States, where he began a rather prosperous professional and family life. He obtained American citizenship, which was certainly easier in those days than it is today, and he led a middle-class life with his wife and first son Eddy. But nostalgia for his homeland eventually gripped him and he decided to return to the land of his ancestors. Like Greeley, who changed his mind a hundred times, Schacht's father first moved to Prussia, in the province of Schleswig, where his second son, Hjalmar, was born on January 22, 1877. A very modest house in the village of Tinglev, now in Denmark, was the place where the greatest financier of the 20th century spent his first months. The Schacht family only stayed there for a short time, before the father Schacht moved to another job, then another town, then another job, then another town - in short, a rather unstable early childhood marked by financial hardship and deprivation.

Finally, the Schacht family moved to Hamburg, where the father found a very low-paying but more permanent job. Hjalmar Schacht spent his childhood, adolescence, and early manhood in the popular, working-class neighborhoods of this large port on the Elbe and North Sea.

He will remain deeply marked by it.

Hamburg is not a cheerful city. When you open your windows - if the weather outside allows it, which is not very often - a low, gray sky is the only prospect. When the Northern European *Schmuddelwetter* ("bad weather") sets in, which is almost every day except for a few weeks in summer, smiles fade from faces, moods become as smoky as the smoke coming out of the chimneys of houses and ships, and one quickly closes the windows to shut oneself in the dreary dampness of the brick houses, lined up in the good Germanic order that prevails in West Prussia. There is no room for fantasy here! Even if one wanted to, there is hardly any possibility of escaping from the gloomy atmosphere. In the Schacht household, every penny is counted. If coal is needed to heat the house, young Hjalmar is given only a few pfennig, and the change, if any, is returned in full to the mother.

So we study. That passes the time and allows to deceive the boredom. All the more so as young Hjalmar is brilliant; what can I say, brilliant... brilliant! When he wants to, he is the first in his class, systematically surpassing the offspring of bourgeois families who, in spite of their private tutors in charge of giving them forceful lessons in algebra and grammar, are no match for Hjalmar or his brother Eddy, and even their younger brother Oluf, a few years younger, and William, the youngest. Can't afford a tutor in the Schacht family? Big deal! The sons are intelligent, hard-working, and the parents instill in them an inflexible sense of duty and responsibility. This is what they are equipped with to face life. With such a background, how could they let themselves be taken advantage of?

In reality, things are a bit more sophisticated: Hjalmar tries to be at the head of the class, but not too much, in order to avoid offending the sensitivities of his less gifted classmates. Not that he's afraid of confrontation: with his brother Eddy, he's not afraid of a fight when it comes to correcting the rich kids who make fun of these poor sons. But blows and bumps don't lead to anything constructive; it's better to act more skilfully and scientifically calculate his results to be in the top third of his class, but not more, so as not to crush too much the stains that surround him and provoke their gratuitous aggression.

By permanently withdrawing into the Aventine of excellence, we forget the human contingencies of poor mortals. With stiffness, we judge without indulgence the weaknesses of which the dunces less well endowed by nature in neurons and synapses are guilty. Thus young Hjalmar, by dint of being right before all the others when it comes to solving third degree equations or disserting on the comparative merits of Goethe and Schiller, ends up developing an acute form of arrogance which will never leave him.

He is superior, he knows it, he makes it known.

But Hjalmar Schacht's youth was not without its wounds. Poverty is a heavy burden to bear and rich kids are often cruel to their less fortunate peers.

The journey of young boys to adolescence and manhood has long been marked by a stage that no longer exists today. Throughout their childhood, boys in the late nineteenth and early twentieth centuries wore short pants, or shorts, even in winter, even in the coldest weather in West Prussia, when the polar winds from the North Sea blew. The first pair of long pants was a decisive initiation ceremony: a boy who no longer went bare-legged was already almost a man. Also, at that time when the smallest piece of fabric was counted and where mass consumption did not exist, ordering from the tailor a pair of long pants for his son was an event of capital importance.

Hjalmar is soon the last in his class to still wear short pants; he pesters his parents to finally own that precious pair of long pants that will make him seem equal to the others. His father finally gives in, but money is so scarce that he can only give his son a pair of pants made of *shoddy*, uncomfortable material made from waste cloth.

"Shacht is in *shoddy*! Schacht is in *shoddy*!" the schoolchildren in the *Gymnasium* courtyard shouted... Hjalmar Schacht clenched his teeth and his fists. A few blows to the head silenced the loudest, but one could not settle their account with a ramrod to all the fools who whispered quips behind his back. The young Schacht knows this. So he swallows his anger and shuts himself up in a haughty silence.

Over the years, Father Schacht's situation improves. He found a job as an accountant in the German branch of an American insurance company. The family was able to move out of the working-class neighborhoods and into a small, cozy house, and then moved to Berlin. The older sons stayed in Hamburg to finish their studies, Hjalmar in philosophy - business studies did not yet exist at that time - and Eddy in medicine. The younger sons Oluf and William follow their parents to Berlin; Oluf successfully studies engineering there.

When they reach manhood, the four boys will integrate the heritage of their youth in very different ways.

Eddy will remain marked by this paternal instability which he will take up again. He practiced medicine all over the world, in Europe and Africa, even settling for a few years in Egypt, near Aswan.

Oluf and William will also be eternal migratory birds, Oluf, in particular in Africa where he will exercise his profession of engineer in several countries before returning to Germany and dying there very young of a heart attack.

As for Hjalmar, he will keep this distant, haughty, arrogant personality, certain of his superiority, convinced that he is always right. In short, he is the archetype of the first of the class that we enjoy hating while recognizing his qualities. However, he has touching, almost sympathetic sides: his detachment from material things, for example. There is no question of Hjalmar Schacht compensating for the frustrations of his youth and the humiliation of *shoddy* pants by wallowing in luxury, once his financial situation is firmly established. No, he remained a stickler for simplicity: dark suits, always the same, hard-collared shirts, always the same, steel-rimmed glasses, trips home by third-class commuter train, even when he was a highly paid investment banker at the Dresdner Bank, the country's leading financial institution. No ostentation, no fantasy, no caprice; on the contrary, whenever he is called upon by the state to save the country from ruin, his first act is to waive his salary or to reduce it by two-thirds. How can we not trust such a man?

What drives Hjalmar Schacht is duty. He knows what he owes to Germany, which gave him his education, his culture, his success as a banker. Germany is the passion of his life.

As for his lack of sensitivity... Unquestionably, it is difficult to discern the slightest trace of sentimentality in the great banker Hjalmar Schacht. Although he wrote no less than twenty-six books, he never revealed his personal emotions, including the dramas or happy events that marked his life. His first marriage to Louise, who would become a rabid pro-Nazi militant unlike himself? He talks about it with an arctic coldness; it is true that their union will end in a divorce. The death of his son, an officer in the Wehrmacht, who disappeared during the war in a prison camp in Russia, coldly shot by a Soviet guard? Just a few words, with a detachment that sends shivers down your spine. The disappearance of his brother Oluf? No expression of grief either. He takes in the children of his two brothers to provide for their education? He attributes this good deed to his sense of family obligations and hardly to the affection he would have for these children, even if he seems to enjoy the company of Eddy's eldest son who will accompany him on several trips. Oh, yes, he does... the smiles of his daughters, born of his second marriage, who welcome him and their mother when he is released from prison, bring tears of deep humanity to his eyes. So somewhere in Schacht there is a sensitive cord that can sometimes vibrate.

In the end, Hjalmar Schacht remains a very tricky personality to pin down. A man of duty, a genius of the economy and finance, he was also a great sportsman and occasionally went mountain running. A curious traveler, as a young man he left for Turkey with his backpack, studied in France and England, visited the United States, and then travelled the world after the war. A Freemason, he was a follower of a rigorous moral rectitude that beat the most demanding of ecclesiastical dogmas... In any case, Schacht is a character of such complexity that he remains very difficult to understand.

Nevertheless, we will remember these outstanding features.

First of all, this brittle, haughty, arrogant character, apparently devoid of any emotional needs, only concerned with being right, incapable of recognizing his wrongs, was undoubtedly perfectly unbearable for those he was in contact with.

However, this man, who allowed Hitler to come to power and thus made possible the most abominable tragedies in human history, because he was moved by the smile of his little girls and openly despised Rolex wearers, could not be totally evil.

Chapter 2. The ambitious

I had some difficult years as a student in London and Paris. I had finished my philosophy studies in Hamburg and wanted to go into business. To do this, I decided to study the works of the great economists in the best libraries in Europe and to write a thesis.

France was not very welcoming for a German student. At the Sorbonne, where I was enrolled, I had to be discreet and hide, as much as I could, my nationality, which did not fail to attract mockery and hostility. The memory of the 1870 war and the annexation by Germany of Alsace-Lorraine were for the French as many reasons to resent us Germans. There was another source of hatred, the importance of which I quickly realized: it was the payment of war reparations to Germany, the considerable cost of which weighed on the health of the French economy. For me, coming from Hamburg, the main commercial port of Europe and a modern and active industrial city, I realized, during my French peregrinations, that this country where I was staying suffered from a certain delay in development compared to Germany.

I learned three lessons from this.

The first is that withdrawal into oneself inevitably increases the difficulties of promoting economic development. Germany, in fact, since the end of the conflict, had adopted a policy resolutely open to the outside world, massively exporting the products of its factories to other European countries and facing competition from other exporters. France, on the other hand, had pursued a much more endogenous policy, taking advantage of its vast colonial empire to extract raw materials and essentially feed its domestic consumption. The result was that France had fewer industries, its products were less elaborate, less modern; it remained a large agricultural country while Germany had already entered the industrial age. The two countries had stimulated their economies in very different ways: France had adopted a fluctuating and poorly designed policy, partly, it is true, to pay war reparations to Germany. But the consequence had been a drying up of trade and a certain lag in industrial development compared with us, the United Kingdom and the United States, the other major competitors in world markets. My country, for its part, had developed as much as it could its foreign trade and protected its domestic market with several protectionist laws. And in this warlike confrontation that did not speak its name, in this real economic conflict, Germany had once again won the battle and dominated its old neighbor.

The second lesson is that the key word when it comes to organizing the economic life of a country is "determination". Determination is what made all the difference. But real determination; not the kind that consists in making a firm speech and then doing nothing or, worse, doing the opposite of what was announced, but the kind that consists in defining an objective to be reached, in following a guideline, and in sticking to it against all odds. During the post-war years of 1870, the German Empire was fortunate to have leaders at the head of its government who showed this determination: Otto von Bismarck, the Iron Chancellor, and then after his resignation in 1890, other politicians of almost the same calibre, or energetic and rather enlightened monarchs. They had a cardinal vision of the future they wanted for the Empire and gave themselves the means to achieve the goal they had set. Meanwhile, in France, the conduct of the country was singularly lacking in that determination which is the key to everything: there was a succession of presidents of the Republic straight out of an opera buffa, such as Félix Faure or Émile Loubet, of presidents of the Council who were concerned above all with preserving their ministerial portfolios and who never succeeded in doing so, and of ministers bogged down by repeated scandals, from the financial disaster of Baron Haussmann's works in Paris, to the widespread corruption of the Suez Canal, to the great fraud of the Panama Canal, not to mention the bank failures that regularly ruined depositors and undermined confidence in the financial system. This determination to direct the destiny of nations for the common good, so present in Berlin and so absent in Paris, had led to a gap between our two countries that seemed almost unbridgeable.

The third lesson was that we Germans no longer had much to fear from our French neighbors. Indeed, the only aspiration of the population in France was revenge: to wage war on the German Empire again, to inflict a rapid defeat, to recover Alsace-Lorraine, and even to take the Saar and the Ruhr as a bonus, in short, to make us pay for the setbacks we had suffered since 1870. This warmongering climate was very unpleasant for the German that I was; but it did not seem very dangerous to me. I am not a specialist in military art, but the insignificant weaknesses of the French economy seemed to me so glaring that they could not fail to have heavy consequences, from near or far, on the warlike apparatus of our turbulent neighbor. If war were to happen one day, I imagined that it would quickly turn to our advantage.

So I left France rather reassured and, passing through London to complete my academic research, I returned to Germany.

I had completed my thesis on The Theoretical Foundations of English Mercantilism. I had already worked in journalism during my studies. I had also published poems in several German journals, which had brought me a certain amount of notoriety. But all of this, despite the prestige I had gained, was far removed from the ambitions I had expressed.

It was time to start a real career, more in line with my aspirations. I was no longer a young boy, I was an accomplished man, and the acquaintance of the great people I had met during my studies or during my work as a journalist had shown me that I had nothing to envy them intellectually, on the contrary. For most of them, their eminent position had only been obtained by virtue of their birth. Being born from the thigh of Jupiter or his cousins was the only rationality for their accession to high responsibilities.

For my part, although I had neither a noble title nor a family fortune, I was no less proud of my family, of my father, a simple accountant in an American insurance company but who had guided his family so well through difficulties, of my mother, who had had the courage to follow my father twice across the immense Atlantic Ocean, of my brother Eddy, who was becoming a famous doctor, or of Oluf, who promised to be a brilliant engineer. I had to show that I was capable of exploiting the qualities I had been endowed with and using the education I had been given.

So I went into business.

I was a quick success, despite my modest origins.

Then, in the summer of 1914, war broke out.

This was my first opportunity to demonstrate my organizational and financial skills for the benefit of the German nation.

In 1903, Hjalmar Schacht was 26 years old. He is a young man who has already studied a lot, traveled, and published, including numerous economic articles, but he is not yet firmly established in life. He has just married Louise, a pretty, athletic, dark-haired young woman who is an avid ice skater. He feels that now is the time to start down the path he has long been preparing for. Schacht is looking for a job in the banking industry. The contacts he had made as a journalist and lecturer on economic subjects enabled him to build up a network of contacts among the leaders of high finance. Through his contacts, he found the job he wanted and began his career as a banker at the country's leading bank, the Dresdner Bank.

With his qualities, his rigor and his working power, he did wonders. In 1909, barely six years after his first steps at the Dresdner Bank, he was appointed director. At the age of 32, he was responsible for the entire branch network of the country's largest bank.

For those who know the banking environment, such a career path is exceptional. Indeed, there is no more traditional environment than banking. At that time, apart from the "well-born" souls either in the nobility or in the very wealthy upper middle class, very few "commoners" reached the holy of holies of the management of large financial establishments. But there were a few: the banks were in full development and their need for young, enterprising executives was immense. Opportunities had to be seized, and Schacht immediately identified how to make his mark among the elite. Even today, reaching the top management of a major bank is still a matter of extraction. Recruitment takes place only in selected circles: Harvard or Skulls and Bones in the United States, the École nationale d'administration (ENA) and the Inspection générale des finances (IGF) in France, Eton and Oxford in Britain. A Hjalmar Schacht, the son of a small accountant, who spent his childhood in the working-class suburbs of Hamburg and graduated from the modest university of Kiel, would probably have no chance today, despite his qualities, whereas at the beginning of the 20th century he was able to enjoy this dazzling career.

In any case, Schacht's success was remarkable. It was also at this time that he was initiated into a Masonic lodge. The future belonged to this young financier, so strict and competent; his dark suit, his hard collars, his steel-rimmed glasses and his always serious air inspired the greatest confidence in all the tycoons of German industry who financed themselves at the Dresdner Bank.

But a young Serbian nationalist militant from Bosnia-Herzegovina and a romantic Viennese prince will change the course of Hjalmar Schacht's life.

Franz Ferdinand of Habsburg, Archduke of Austria, was a man with rather liberal ideas. He was in favor of a certain autonomy for the peoples who lived on the margins of the Austro-Hungarian Empire, such as the Bosnians or the Croats. A man of conviction with a strong character, he had made a love marriage with a strikingly beautiful Czech woman, Countess Sophie Chotek von Chotkowa und Wognin. For five years, this man with a shady character had besieged, begged and pleaded with Emperor Franz Joseph, ruler of Austria-Hungary, to obtain permission to marry Sophie, with whom he was madly in love. His tenacity overcame the emperor's reluctance to allow an exception to the principle that a crown prince of the House of Habsburg should marry a member of a ruling family in Europe, which was not the case with Sophie. But Franz Ferdinand was in love, and it is said that the power of this feeling sometimes overturns the reason of state. The emperor, however, imposed a morganatic marriage: Sophie would never be empress, and during official ceremonies she would have to stay away from her husband, the future emperor. Sophie and Franz Ferdinand finally got married without any member of the imperial family deigning to attend the ceremony, and they became one of the most united couples in Europe, leading a rather secluded existence, raising their four children, and indulging their common passion, botany.

At the beginning of the summer of 1914, when they went to Sarajevo, the capital of Bosnia-Herzegovina, where Franz Ferdinand was to inaugurate a museum, the two spouses knew that the trip was not without risk because attacks had been multiplying for several months. Nevertheless, they went together: there was no way they could travel without each other.

A very beautiful day, this June 28, 1914.

Franz Ferdinand and Sophie got into their car and, with a strong escort, made their way through the streets of the old town, in the midst of a rather friendly crowd, on their way to the reception organized in their honor. But Serbian nationalists have fomented an attack. One of the conspirators threw a grenade in the direction of the car of the princely couple. The bomb misses its target and explodes in the middle of the procession, a few meters away.

François-Ferdinand and Sophie are unharmed.

In the general panic, the cars rush towards the governor's residence. There, people came to their senses. François-Ferdinand was shocked, but as the Archduke, heir to the Habsburg Empire, he could not be impressed by anarchists. He decides to go to the hospital to comfort the wounded. With Sophie close to him, they set off again into the streets of Sarajevo, crowded with people who were taken aback by the attack. In front of the hospital, the crowd is dense, the curious mingling with the families who want to check on their loved ones and the soldiers who are trying to restore order.

The car of François-Ferdinand stops in the middle of the populace. It was written that the Archduke would not survive the day.

Among the crowd, a few members of the conspirators pass by, dejected by their failure, and disperse to return to their lair. Gavrilo Princip, a young Serbian student and nationalist activist, is one of them. This kid who is not yet 20 years old carries a revolver.

The opportunity is too good.

Before the escort, entangled in the crowd, could intervene, Gavrilo Princip jumped on the footboard of the car and unloaded his six bullets on Sophie and Franz Ferdinand.

The Archduke died with his last words of love to the woman he loved so much: "Sophie, Sophie don't die, stay alive for our children."

Can Sophie hear him? Probably not. She exhales in turn before arriving at the hospital.

The old lovers are the first victims of a terrible domino effect; In the following days, Austria-Hungary declares war on Serbia (July 28), Russia, ally of Serbia, decrees the general mobilization (July 30), then Germany after the expiration of the ultimatum launched to Russia to stop "all measures of war" declares war on it (August 1) as well as on France (August 3), then the United Kingdom to Germany (August 3), until the whole of Europe decreed general mobilization and left, with the flower in the gun, to relieve its age-old hatreds against its neighbors.

François-Ferdinand of Habsburg, heir to the imperial crown of Austria-Hungary, did not see the war that would bloody Europe for more than four years, from 1914 to 1918. This romantic man who only wished to live in peace, with his sweet Sophie on his arm, in the midst of the children he cherished and the roses he cultivated with passion, certainly did not imagine that he would write his name in history like the prince whose death triggered one of the most appalling butcheries in the history of humanity.

Gavrilo Princip did not see the horrible butchery either. Following his arrest, he was not sentenced to death, because he was under 20 years of age at the time of his fatal act and the Austro-Hungarian Penal Code excluded capital punishment below that age. But he was imprisoned in the fortress of Theresienstadt, (kingdom of Bohemia), Sophie's country. He was locked up in a cell without a roof, which left him exposed to the elements, rain, snow, cold or heat. Already suffering from tuberculosis during his imprisonment, he died in April 1918; he was 25 years old. The world war was not yet over; more than one and a half million young men of his age would die on the battlefields after Gavrilo Princip's death, before the hostilities ended a few months later, in November 1918, with a total death toll of nine million.

Hjalmar Schacht, on the other hand, saw the First World War. Not as a soldier - he was discharged because of his short-sightedness - but as a financier, his field of excellence.

And for him, the war is a great opportunity.

For the first time, it will be able to demonstrate that it can solve questions of state, political issues, governmental problems.

For the first time, he will also be confronted with those obtuse civil servants with thick eyebrows and low foreheads whose existence he will enjoy upsetting for the rest of his life with his revolutionary ideas.

The scene takes place in Brussels, at the end of 1914. The German armies, passing through Belgium, have overrun the French forces. The north and east of France were invaded and the front had stabilized on the Somme and the Marne, less than a hundred kilometers from Paris. The infantry divisions, on both the French and German sides, were buried in a complex network of trenches and fortifications, defended by barbed wire and protected by sandbags. The infantrymen died in the mud and the cold of winter, which were as much feared as the enemy's machine gun fire. The soldiers would remain face to face for four years, gutting each other for a few meters of ground.

Belgium was completely occupied by Germany. This small country saw the Kaiser's armies pass through and fought as best it could, but the disproportion of forces was such that the German advance was only slowed down for a few days. The German Empire, always so well organized, set up an occupation administration in Belgium to manage the country and make requisitions to supply the German divisions stationed there. To take care of the finances of this vast military administration and, beyond that, of the finances of the whole country, because the Belgian government had gone into exile in London and left the power in disarray, a financier was needed.

And why not this remarkable *Herr Doktor* Hjalmar Schacht, director of the Dresdner Bank?

Schacht immediately accepted the offer, made two months after the outbreak of war, to go to Brussels to administer the finances of the occupying forces and the occupied Belgian state. There, he took orders from Karl von Lumm, an old-school Prussian civil servant who, in civilian life, was a member of the board of the Reichsbank, the central bank of the German Empire.

Obviously, with Hjalmar Schacht's usual stiffness and air of superiority, things did not go well between Lumm and his subordinate. Schacht had already opposed Lumm's plan to change the Belgian currency, because he thought it unnecessary and costly. But Lumm overruled his young collaborator and the currency change took place. Nothing particularly favorable resulted from this operation, and Schacht did not fail to make this known.

Lumm didn't appreciate it.

And now Schacht is asking for a pass to go and eat in the officers' mess? This pipsqueak will learn to respect German discipline!

- *Herr* Lumm, I respectfully request that I be allowed to eat in the officers' mess," Hjalmar Schacht asks, looking as haughty and full of arrogance as usual.

- No way, Schacht!" his superior replied curtly. Civilian employees are not allowed to eat with the military. The regulations are very clear about this!

- *Herr* Lumm, I would respectfully point out that the officers' mess is nearby. We would only save time and money with this permission.

- You're not thinking about it, Schacht! The military will not accept it! And in any case, it would require the authorization of Governor General Colmar von der Goltz who commands the military place.

- Very well, *Herr* Lumm. Let's send him a note," replies Hjalmar Schacht.

- I'm not going to bother Governor General Goltz about a lunch matter, *Doktor* Schacht. Let there be no further discussion of this matter!

But Hjalmar Schacht was not one to give in. The request was submitted to the head of the Foreign Affairs section, Oscar von der Lancken-Wakenitz. Another obtuse and stupidly disciplined Prussian official, as Schacht was so fond of.

- No, *Doktor* Schacht," said Lancken-Wakenitz, "I do not see how we can allow a civilian to go to the officers' mess to eat. And I refuse to disturb someone as eminent as Governor General Goltz just to satisfy the wish of a subordinate. After all, you only have the title of *Doktor* here, *Herr* Schacht!"

- Very well, gentlemen," Schacht replied calmly and firmly. If you really believe that this request cannot be submitted by you to Governor General Goltz, then I will ask him myself.

- But... do you know him?

- Of course. I did not want to make an exception to the chain of command and that is why I made the request. But since apparently another method is preferable...

And Hjalmar Schacht went to ask for an audience with Governor General Goltz, who welcomed him with open arms and immediately invited him to dine with him in the officers' mess. Lumm and Lancken-Wakenitz were both stunned and furious...

But Schacht's arrogance, intelligence and determination were to be put to use in other, more serious matters. In his capacity as financial advisor for Belgium, he tackled his first major monetary and economic problem: requisitions.

Schacht noted that the Belgian economy was in a state of virtual deadlock. Not because of the destruction caused by the war, because there was hardly any fighting in Belgium and the country, even under German administration, was perfectly able to function normally, but because the military requisitions intended to maintain the occupying forces completely blocked economic exchanges.

Requisitions were in fact carried out in an authoritarian manner. The military intendance seized all the supplies the army needed: fodder for the animals, agricultural production to feed the men and the cattle, horses to pull the cannons and to provide the cavalry's remount, construction materials, etc. In exchange, it gave the farmers, industrialists and merchants from whom the requisitions were made "requisition vouchers", a sort of "voucher". In exchange, it gave farmers, industrialists and shopkeepers who were requisitioned "requisition vouchers", a kind of security that was to be reimbursed one day by the Belgian State. These "vouchers" constitute a kind of quasi-money, since they are exchangeable and redeemable and can be passed from hand to hand, like normal money. In theory, all this should work well and not prevent the Belgian economy from producing goods and services at its usual rate.

But it is not.

Indeed, Schacht notices two phenomena.

The first is that agricultural and industrial production falls, at least in appearance. Indeed, farmers and industrialists either stopped producing goods that could be seized during the requisitions, or they hid them and sold them on the black market. Thus, the requisitions are more and more difficult for the German army, and the civilian population, for its part, suffers from shortages and the increasing cost of goods.

The second phenomenon is that money, or at least official money, in short, that which constitutes the oil in the gears of the economic machine and makes possible the exchange of goods and services, tends to disappear from circulation. Schacht relates this to an axiom that is well known to economists and that he studied during his years in London and Paris. It is the old adage: "Bad money drives out good money." In other words, when two currencies are in circulation, households, businesses, and even banks, will tend to hoard the good money, the one that inspires confidence, and will strive to dispose of the bad money, the one that does not inspire confidence, at all costs. Requisition notes" do not inspire confidence. Consequently, those who hold these "vouchers" try to get rid of them, while the real money, the official money, is kept under the mattress or in the safe. Result: economic stagnation, inflation, shortages...

A Lumm or a Lancken-Wakenitz can live with such a situation. After all, they are only civil servants, they are not there to shake up the established order. They do what unimaginative civil servants or politicians usually do: continue as before, without changing anything.

But not Hjalmar Schacht.

His intelligence is revolted when he sees that no one, for lack of having correctly analyzed the situation, does anything to modify this established order, which seems to be installed for eternity, or in any case until the end of the German occupation, that is to say an indeterminate duration... Schacht is convinced that he can make sure that the economy functions normally, for the greatest benefit of both the German military and the Belgian civilian population

For this, there are two prerequisites.

First of all, the hierarchy: Lumm and Lancken-Wakewitz. Fortunately, the episode in the officers' mess showed them that he, Hjalmar Schacht, was not made of soft wood and that he had connections in high places. So he would have a free hand in this respect. To a certain extent, at least.

The other prerequisite is the method. How to turn the tide of an economic machine on a dead-end street? This is where Schacht's genius and determination to act will find expression. Hjalmar Schacht's idea was to do away with the "requisition vouchers" and pay the occupying army in real money. In this way, the economy would recover as it had before the war. But the catch is that there are no funds available within the military administration to pay for the goods the army needs. Moreover, the Reich will certainly not release any. The German Empire was all the more reluctant to provide this funding because the armistice agreement with the Belgian state duly provided that the latter was to bear the expenses of the occupation. But the Belgian state was ruined, bloodless, without a penny to its name...

How to do it?

Schacht has a brilliant idea.

In these adverse conditions, the only solution is for the Belgian State to launch a loan from its population, which has so well hoarded official money under its mattresses! Thus, the Belgian administration will have funds in authentic money to pay directly for the requisitions; farmers and industrialists will be able to be paid with real money; thanks to this incentive, the population will start working again; it will start producing goods again without systematically destining them to the black market; finally, the German army will be satisfied because the requisitions, henceforth paid on the nose by the Belgian State, will be facilitated. And the icing on the cake was that the economic activity thus re-established would bring in tax revenues that would allow the Belgian state to pay the rent on the loans... In short, a virtuous circle of economic growth would be reborn, despite the German occupation.

Hjalmar Schacht, when he presented this plan to his superiors, received a cold reception.

He doesn't care.

He is right, he knows it, and he lets it be known.

Without respite, Schacht set to work to convince all levels of the administration of the relevance of his plan. The challenge was immense, but his determination was total. There is no difficulty he considers insurmountable. However, sometimes obstacles arise that are impossible to overcome. One of them is that there is no longer a Belgian state! The Belgian government is in exile in London and it is certainly not going to approve, from England, a loan intended for the Germans, organized by a German, even if it appears that the Belgian population could benefit from it.

It's a dead end.

But not for the devil's banker.

Hjalmar Schacht finds a way around it. There is no longer a Belgian state? So be it! But there are still the nine provinces that make up the Kingdom of Belgium, each of which has its own elected officials. He made the rounds of the nine regional prefectures; each time, he had to deploy all his strength of conviction to convince his interlocutors. Fortunately, he had a perfect command of the French language, the result of his years spent in Paris. And Hjalmar Schacht succeeded. The nine provinces all agreed to guarantee the loan in place of the Belgian state. Schacht even learned news that made him very happy: certain channels of communication seemed to have remained active between the Belgian provinces and the government in exile in London. The latter, informed of Schacht's operation, would have been convinced of his interest. According to the rumours circulating, he approved the principle of this loan and gave instructions to encourage its success, or at least not to hinder its launch...

Finally, after several weeks of preparation, the loan launch is ready.

It is a success.

Everything worked as Schacht had planned. Economic life is reborn in Belgium.

As he said, he was right!

Schacht triumphs.

He spent the entire war in Brussels managing the finances of the occupation administration under Lumm's orders; difficult years, despite this initial success. The jealousy, mistrust, and bitterness of the obtuse civil servants under whose rule he had to work were not easy to bear for a personality like his.

He eventually resigned from his position a few months before the end of the war.

But Lumm is not quite finished with him. Schacht has overshadowed him for almost four years? Now that he is leaving, this arrogant character will pay and Lumm will gladly present the bill...

Lumm brought out an old story: during the currency change that he, Lumm, had ordered at the beginning of the occupation, and that Hjalmar Schacht had disapproved of, a fraudulent operation was ordered by Schacht. Indeed, Schacht, a former member of the Dresdner Bank, would have had stocks of new banknotes unduly attributed to this establishment, which had not been approved by him, Lumm...

- *Herr* Lumm," Hjalmar Schacht shouted, "you know that this allocation of banknotes was regular! It was simply intended to supply the branches of the Dresdner Bank so that they could participate in the monetary change and continue their activity normally!

- Yes, *Doktor* Schacht... but weren't you just the branch manager at the Dresdner Bank?

- This has absolutely nothing to do with anything, *Herr* Lumm! The delivery of banknotes to the Dresdner Bank was approved by the Governor General's office itself!

- But it was you who asked for it, *Doktor* Schacht... it's rather embarrassing... considering your former position in this bank, it would have been better if this request had been made by someone else...

- Even so, *Herr* Lumm! There are no irregularities here! If you feel that I am to blame, I will formally request that a disciplinary investigation be initiated against me! It will establish that no fraud has been committed!

- Ah, dear *Doktor* Schacht, unfortunately this is no longer possible. You resigned two days ago... and the administrative instruction no. AWT-1452 of the manual of the occupation authorities excludes, in this case, that a disciplinary investigation can be initiated at the request of a resigned employee...

No investigation was conducted and the rumor of fraud during his tenure in Brussels followed Hjalmar Schacht for a long time.

Upon his return to Berlin, Schacht resumed his duties as branch manager of the Dresdner Bank. But now he had his sights set higher: several positions on the bank's board of directors became available. One of them was bound to be his. Moreover, the son of the president of the Dresdner Bank, an incompetent and lazy man, has been appointed to it; yet another pass to a fraud by the magic of his birth alone. It is therefore necessary that he, Hjalmar Schacht, whose qualities as a financier are now renowned in the most powerful business circles in Germany, quickly obtains this position. He deserves it! But weeks passed and the appointment did not come. Schacht finally asked for an interview with the president, who, somewhat embarrassed, referred him to his son, the notoriously incompetent smoker.

- *Herr* administrator, I came to ask you about my appointment to the board, asks Schacht.

- Ah, *Doktor* Schacht! I think you'll have to be a little patient. You see, I took the initiative to postpone your arrival at the council," replied the president's son.

- May I ask the reason for this decision?

- Uh... actually... I'm afraid that your presence is a nuisance to me...

Hjalmar Schacht, after a moment of surprise, bursts into laughter.

- Well, if this is the effect my collaboration has on you and the board, I think the only solution for you is to accept my resignation!

Ambition is not always easy to satisfy; Hjalmar Schacht learned this several times at his own expense: you annoy some people, you offend others, you arouse the jealousy or hatred of others...

But the financier has tasted power.

This is what he is aiming at now.

Chapter 3. The savior

Germany owes its renaissance to me.

The war had made my country suffer: on the Eastern and Western fronts, a whole generation of young men had disappeared in a foul soup of iron and blood. But the war was essentially fought outside our borders. Our factories were ready to operate, our mines ready to supply the ore to feed them, and our fields ready to be sown again to produce the food for the workers who were ready to work. Germany, in fact, was intact, ready to regain its place among the great world powers.

It should have been so.

This was not the case.

Through the fault of weak and spineless leaders, through the fault of foreign powers whose only goal was to ruin my country for centuries and centuries, through the fault of a few selfish and greedy unscrupulous monopolists, ready to sacrifice their countrymen to enrich themselves, Germany could have disappeared in the chaos of a monetary crisis without precedent in the history of civilization, and which has never happened again since.

Thanks to me, she survived.

Thanks to this crisis, I became world famous: I became the man who restored Germany's pride and prosperity.

Until my appointment as Reichskommissar für die Währung (Reich Commissioner for the Currency) in 1923, the post-war period for my country was a long series of humiliations, hopes and disappointments, and even deep attacks on our dignity and integrity.

For my part, I continued my business career. My reputation as a banker and financier was well established, and after I left the Dresdner Bank, there was no shortage of offers. When the government came to me to solve its intractable monetary situation, I was the mainstay of the Danat Bank board of directors, which was to make a name for itself many years after my departure, when the resounding bankruptcy that marked the beginning of Hitler's rise to power took place. But I was more concerned with the situation in my country than with banking transactions; I became increasingly indifferent to finance as my country sank into a crisis that was to prove fatal. Indeed, the economic crisis was coupled with a social crisis, with riots, rebellions and strikes that were spreading disorder throughout the territory we had left. The economic crisis was tripled by a political crisis with conspiracies, coup attempts and a government that suffered from recurrent weakness. And Europe watched Germany sink into nothingness with barely concealed delight, especially on the French side. On the contrary, as soon as it was a question of pushing our heads a little further into the mud, France immediately replied "Present!", as it did when it invaded the industrial provinces of the Ruhr on the right bank of the Rhine without any legitimate reason.

But that was no surprise to me.

With the possible exception of American President Woodrow Wilson, all the leaders of the countries against which Germany had fought loyally had decided that defeat was not enough: Germany had to be kept in such a state of underdevelopment that she would never again represent a "danger" to Europe. This reasoning was pure madness! How can one imagine keeping sixty million men and women, in the heart of Europe, in the state of humiliated beggars, without thinking that one day they will react and revolt? And then seek revenge for the frustrations that were imposed on them without rationality?

In 1919, I took part in a round of negotiations with other German industrialists and financiers in The Hague, Netherlands, about economic reparations and chemical deliveries to our victors. The French general who chaired the meeting made it clear to me that if we were ever to regain a modicum of respect in Europe, we would never owe it to anyone but ourselves, and certainly not to the Allies, who were thinking mainly of crushing us under their heels.

The German delegation stayed in a shabby hotel, with two or three people per room, with beds infested with bedbugs. Police officers supervised our every move. The food we were served deserved only one description: execrable. As for the room in which the meetings were held, around the table only two chairs were reserved for the German delegation, while there were twenty of us; it should be noted that in the camp opposite, each member of the Allied delegation had a seat at his disposal.

I went to find the French general.

- General, our conditions of stay here are simply unacceptable! Our accommodation is not a hotel, but a last class boozer, we cannot move around without a lot of police harassment, and in this room we cannot sit down! For the sake of our discussions, this has to stop!

- Sir," he threw me in a contemptuous tone without even giving me a glance, "don't forget that your country has lost the war!

And he turned away from me without paying the slightest attention.

The conditions given to Germany after the armistice were simply iniquitous; whole sections of our territory were annexed, by France, by Poland, by a country created for the occasion, Czechoslovakia, a curious assemblage of Czechs, Slovaks, Germans, Hungarians and Austrians. No one thought to take into account that in these regions, good German families had been living for centuries and had established themselves there. In Alsace, East Prussia, and the Sudetenland, these good, peaceful people had, through their efforts and their innate sense of organization, transformed these regions into pleasant and prosperous countryside.

In economic terms, the conditions imposed on Germany were totally absurd. The Allies imposed on us the payment of war damages of an astronomical amount, but without allowing us to develop the industrial apparatus that would allow us to produce the wealth to pay for them. Our situation was in every way comparable to that of an unemployed person who has no hope of ever finding work again, and on whose head a debt of a million gold marks is imposed. And if he wants to find a job anyway, he is forbidden to do so! And if he argues that he can't pay, he is punished!

These conditions were simply an insult to common sense.

And so it happened: Germany plunged into an economic, social and political crisis that brought it to the brink of collapse.

The government called me to the rescue.

It was November 13, 1923.

Less than five years later, I had stabilized the value of the currency, curbed inflation, renegotiated Germany's debt and war damages, and restored confidence in my country.

I, Hjalmar Schacht!

I bet that this French general, if I had asked him for a chair at that moment, would have advanced me a chair himself! In person!

Stresemann was not a man of decision.

In 1929, at the age of 51, Gustav Stresemann, who was in poor health and reformed during the Great War because of a kidney disease, was appointed Chancellor, or Prime Minister, by President Friedrich Ebert, the new president of the German Republic, which was called the Weimar Republic, in the summer of 1923. Gustav Stresemann was a pragmatic man, devoted to the public cause, but a messy one, and a pitiful economist. He managed his personal affairs in an abominably calamitous way and died ruined, covered in debt.

When Stresemann came to power, chaos reigned in the country. Foreign Minister Walther Rathenau had been assassinated a few months earlier; extreme right and left-wing groups were springing up everywhere; hyperinflation was reaching new heights, ruining the entire German middle class as well as the old traditional nobility; and unemployment was rampant.

The final collapse of Germany has never seemed so close.

It would take a charismatic leader, a Bismarck, a Metternich to get Germany out of this hell. Gustav Stresemann is certainly not that person.

However, on November 13, 1923, faced with the insurrectionary situation that was spreading in Germany, he finally decided to take two essential measures.

First, he passed a law that day that gave him full power to suppress disorder, riots and attempted coups in the country. Four days earlier, on November 9, 1923, Adolf Hitler tried to seize power in Munich by force, but failed. It was only a postponement.

Then Stresemann, who had known Hjalmar Schacht for almost twenty years, managed to convince this successful banker, who was comfortably settled in his business life and who had a network of very useful financial relations in England and the United States, to take on the duties of Reich Commissioner for Currency. On November 13, 1923, Hjalmar Schacht endorsed his letter of appointment.

But there was a catch: there was no such position as Reich Commissioner for Currency. Neither in the Ministry of Economics and Finance nor in the Reichsbank was there any provision for a Reich Commissioner for Currency. Nowhere is there an administration to assist him, no premises to house him, no means for him to carry out his work. His powers are not mentioned in any law, decree or regulation. Does this power even exist? Already, it would be hard to name the real powers of the Minister of Finance or the Governor of the Reichsbank: their disarray in the face of the monetary crisis is so desperate...

By the way, what is this crisis?

In order to understand what the economic crisis after the First World War meant for the German population, today's reader has to go back a few years. In the 20th century, in the 1970s, the developed economies of, for example, the United States, France, the United Kingdom, most European states and some Asian countries experienced episodes of high inflation, in the range of 10 to 15 percent per year. Around the same time, emerging economies (Argentina, Mexico, Brazil, Turkey, etc.) experienced years of rampant inflation. One of the most emblematic examples is Argentina in the 1980s. This country, which had just emerged from a military dictatorship and a highly regulated economy, was experimenting with democracy and the transition to a market economy. Argentina was faced with years of dramatic hyperinflation: around +5,000% in 1989 and +1,400% in 1990.

Next to these impressive figures, the European inflation of the same period, with its +10 to +15%, was a pleasant faribole.

The purchasing power of the Argentine peso, between 1980 and 1990, was divided by one hundred and fifty! Not less than one hundred and fifty! To take a European comparison, a family that had savings of the equivalent of one hundred and fifty thousand euros in 1980, enough to buy a small apartment in a provincial town, would only have the equivalent of one thousand euros in 1990, barely enough to pay for the repair of its old car.

This shows the truly catastrophic nature of these episodes of hyperinflation for the standard of living of the population: only ruin and desolation emerge, not to mention the disorders that the harshness of life does not fail to provoke: social unrest, strikes, riots and long queues in front of soup kitchens.

Well, despite the apparent seriousness of the crisis in Argentina, all this is nothing. The Argentine drama or those of the same period appear truly microscopic compared to what happened in Germany after the First World War.

Let's remember the results of the Argentine crisis: the peso fell to one hundred and fiftieth of its value.

Here is the balance sheet of the German crisis: the mark-paper had fallen to the five hundred billionth part of its value.

Such a figure is very difficult for the human mind to embrace. Perhaps it is clearer to express this magnitude in numbers, with a more or less stable reference, i.e. gold.

In 1918, one gold mark was worth two paper marks.

This same mark-gold was worth, in 1923, one thousand billion paper marks, that is to say in figures, 1,000,000,000,000 paper marks!

In five years, the value of the currency issued by the Reichsbank, expressed in gold equivalent, thus increased from two to one thousand billion; to repeat the previous comparison, this is a devaluation in Argentina, but multiplied by a factor of several tens of millions.

These staggering figures seem to have a more astronomical than economic dimension. Yet they represent what German families experienced on a daily basis between 1918 and 1923. The image of the wheelbarrows of money needed for the smallest purchase, the fable of the prices of basic consumer goods, such as bread, which doubled or tripled during the day, the weekly salary which was barely enough to pay for a meal in the most modest of restaurants, the ruin of a whole people of small savers, of old bourgeois families and of the traditional nobility, all this is the sad reality of post-war German society.

What caused this hyperinflation? Several factors combined to cause it. First of all, the conditions imposed on Germany at the time of the war's end were an outright murder: in addition to the loss of economically prosperous territories to the winners of the conflict, the amount of reparations to be paid to the Allies was such that almost all the wealth produced by the country had to be devoted to them. There was almost nothing left for the population itself. So the solution to keep a subsistence economy going was to pursue a lax monetary policy and to print money. In this way, the population had the resources for a minimum of economic exchange. But this was obviously a very short-sighted policy, dictated by circumstances and carried out in a particularly clumsy manner.

It was all the more clumsy because it was led by men whose authority was so weak that they could not, or did not know, how to oppose the profiteers who were blooming on this historic crisis, like flowers blooming on a pile of manure. Systematically, in economic history, crises are the soil on which speculators, traders, and specialists in dubious finance multiply like maggots in a carrion. These people have no interest in seeing an end to inflation or, more broadly, an end to the crisis in which they are swimming comfortably, like mud fish in murky swamp water; on the contrary, their level of enrichment increases according to the intensity of the effects of the crisis. They know, for example, how to take advantage of currency volatility. It is not very complicated, and it is not very difficult to stop them either, but it requires political will, technical ability and determination. But the leaders who preceded Hjalmar Schacht at the helm of the German economy were singularly lacking in all three.

To all this were added other epiphenomena: the circulation of parallel currencies, emergency "bonds" and other quasi-currencies issued by numerous official bodies and even by private companies, outside of any control by the Reichsbank, the issue of a new currency, the rentenmark - whose value was not really known at first, whether it should be indexed to rye (yes, the cereal!...), real estate or other types of assets -, black market currencies, which annihilated the Reichsbank's exchange control measures...

When Hjalmar Schacht took up his post as Reich Commissioner for Money, the task was immense, insurmountable; and the means at his disposal were strictly zero.

But nothing can discourage Dr. Hjalmar Schacht.

First, we need to find space.

At the Reichsbank? No way. Hostility towards him was immediate. This Reich Commissioner for currency is nothing more than an intruder who wants to step on the toes of the Central Bank... Let him not hope to settle here!

At the Ministry of Finance? Oh, my God!... How embarrassing... The Minister of Finance would be very happy to receive Dr. Schacht, but unfortunately, the Ministry has no available premises commensurate with the prestige of this eminent visitor... Impossible to receive him under these conditions which are not worthy of him! Let him knock at another door...

They do not yet know Hjalmar Schacht.

This one, while leaving the Ministry of Finance, notices in the courtyard a door framed by windows blacked out by newspaper. He called a guard, asked for the keys and opened the door. It is a dusty and humid shed.

- *Herr Doktor*?" the guard ventured. As you can see, it's just a storage room...

- Who uses this place?" asks Schacht.

- The cleaning ladies. See, they dry their mops there...

- Clear out this room," Schacht ordered. Set up two tables, two chairs and a telephone. I'll come tomorrow with my secretary. Have everything ready!

That's the first thing that's been taken care of. He has an official office at the Ministry of Finance. Of course, he is no longer the host of the prestigious, comfortable premises, decorated with warm woodwork and sumptuous Persian carpets, which were the usual setting for his work as a great banker, but this maid's room will do the trick!

Now we need staff.

- I'm coming with my secretary," Schacht tells the chief of staff at the Ministry of Finance. How much can you pay her?

- Two hundred marks per month.

- Ridiculous! At Danat Bank, she earns six hundred. And my salary, how much is it?

- Four hundred marks, *Herr Doktor*," replied the chief of staff, a little embarrassed, but inwardly delighted to inform this great banker of the paltry amount of his emoluments.

- Very well! Give her my four hundred marks in addition to her two hundred. That way she won't lose anything.

- But you, *Herr Doktor* Schacht? Are you going to work for nothing?

- What you offer me is insignificant compared to what I used to earn. So I will work for nothing, but give my secretary six hundred marks!

An office, a telephone, a secretary... a dose of genius and a lot of determination... The Schacht plan is set up.

But what is this plan? For the time being, just as he always did, at the Dresdner Bank, the Danat Bank or elsewhere, Schacht arrives early at his office in the Ministry of Finance, in a dark suit, hard collared shirt, small steel rimmed glasses. He stays late, very late, and then goes home by third-class commuter train.

And in the meantime, what is *Herr Doktor* Schacht doing?

He smokes.

He smokes a cigar.

All day.

The dresses of *Fräulein* Steffeck, his secretary who shares the maids' storeroom with him, reek of tobacco.

Is that all?

Yes, that's all.

For the moment, Hjalmar Schacht smokes and thinks.

Then he grabs the phone. And starts to call. For hours and hours, until late at night, he discusses, consults, pleads, defends, explains.

Finally, it is ready.

Yes, he is ready, but is the government and the country ready?

The paltry means at his disposal and the difficulties he faced in setting up his office showed that no one believed in the mission he had been given. The Reichsbank reacted very badly to the fact that Schacht wanted to take over a power that belonged exclusively to the Central Bank. As for Stresemann, the chancellor who had appointed Hjalmar Schacht to his post, there was little support to be expected from him: this man was incapable of real authority. Accustomed to perpetually playing both sides of the fence, wishing to please everyone without upsetting anyone, he ended up being universally despised and resigned as chancellor ten days after Schacht's appointment.

So, not much to expect in terms of government support.

The country's membership was another problem; Hjalmar Schacht, before revealing his intentions, took the precaution of surrounding himself with guarantees. A bit like in Belgium, when he had toured the nine Belgian provinces to set up his war loan, Schacht contacted the deputies, especially those of the peasant parties, to ensure that there would be no difficulties on their side. He knew that the industrialists and bankers, in other words, those of whom he had been a member a few weeks earlier, would be fiercely opposed. He knew them well, these big businessmen, bogged down in their personal interests and their fierce greed, openly despising the notion of the public good: before his appointment as Reich Commissioner for the currency, he was a member of some sixty boards of directors of the largest capitalist institutions in Germany.

But monetary stabilization is the priority, and Schacht, as he likes to remind us, has no qualms about it.

He is right, he knows it, and he lets it be known.

And he launches his operation.

First of all, the uncontrolled circulation of money had to be stopped. Schacht had the Reichsbank forbid the repayment of parallel currencies, the "emergency bonds" issued by private banks, by large companies and by state bodies that were not the central bank. This decision immediately drew the wrath of these issuers of "emergency bonds", in particular the anger of the large industrialists and bankers who were his constituents. Schacht took part in several meetings of the employers' association, where he was subjected to a barrage of harsh criticism and even threats. But he remained inflexible. He had decided. There is no room for discussion. Let those who had issued these "emergency bonds" deal with the holders: the Reichsbank was henceforth forbidden to pay out a single pfennig to repay them.

The second priority was speculators, traders, banks and agencies that took advantage of the monetary disorder to enrich themselves. Schacht decided to strangle them. He knew that many of them were taking out loans with the Reichsbank to finance their speculations, in particular short sales and purchases of currencies, especially American dollars. Schacht had these loans prohibited overnight, even though all these speculators had open positions that they had to finance at all costs. But too bad for them! The Reichsbank would only trade in dollars at the official rate, the rate at which Schacht wanted to stabilize the currency. All requests for credit at other rates were refused. Traders, speculators, financiers are ruined, washed out, laminated? *Schade*! No way to give in. The interest of the country comes first!

In a few weeks, Schacht achieved what no one had even managed to imagine in his most unlikely dreams: he magically stabilized the currency. Inflation crystallized at around 10%.

The battle is won. The country is calming down.

But it's not quite over yet. The German economy is in a catastrophic state of decay. A more profound monetary reform was needed to put it back on a firmer footing. Schacht decided that the currency had to be changed, to do away with the surreal mark-paper, whose bills in circulation, expressed in billions, were overloaded with zeros. The Reichsmark had to be recreated, a currency that would inspire confidence. To do this, he needed a position other than Reich Commissioner for Currency, with more than a secretary for all the staff in a storeroom at the Ministry of Finance.

President of the Reichsbank: this is the position he would need.

Old Rudolf Havenstein, that archaic conservative who was president and had done absolutely nothing effective to curb hyperinflation, had the good sense to die suddenly while Schacht was carrying out monetary stabilization.

This was probably the best inspiration Havenstein had to help resolve the crisis, because his succession as head of the Reichsbank was now open. Friedrich Ebert, the President of the Republic, began to look for a replacement. Logically, he had Schacht in mind, who was struggling at the time to stabilize the currency and put an end to inflation.

But the Reichsbank Board did not want Hjalmar Schacht at its head. They would prefer someone else, a deputy, a discreet and malleable economist, a professor of economics who had published a number of learned and soporific books on monetary matters. To prevent Schacht's appointment, the members of the board spread rumors about his rigidity, his character... and his honesty. Wasn't there an old affair in Belgium when Schacht was advisor for monetary affairs? A fraud for the bank from which he came, the Dresdner Bank, which his superior, a man named Lumm, formerly of the Reichsbank, had uncovered? Lumm had been head of the Reichsbank's research department, so he must have been a shrewd man... and he didn't think much of this arrogant poseur Schacht...

Hjalmar Schacht was not born yesterday. At his request, at the time of his appointment as currency commissioner, an internal investigation was conducted into the alleged fraud reported by Lumm. Chancellor Stresemann personally wrote him a letter exonerating him from all charges. In a meeting with President Friedrich Ebert, he held up this document.

- Mr. Chairman, as you will see from this letter from the Chancellor himself, these insinuations are slander!

- Very well, I'll take note of that. *Herr* Schacht," the President asked, "you have already done a lot for the stability of our currency. But we still have to achieve definitive results. Do you expect to achieve this stabilization?

- Mr. Chairman, I have enough confidence in myself to believe that I will get through this task! I will do it with all my might.

The appointment of the President of the Central Bank was not, however, a mere formality. When he consulted the Reichsbank Board, President Ebert was rebuffed: an expert report by the members of the Board themselves came out unanimously against Schacht. In addition, the Reichsbank's advisory board, which included some forty leading German businessmen, also voted against him: thirty-seven votes against, three votes for: they did not appreciate being so badly affected by Schacht's decisions on monetary stabilization. Conversely, the Chamber of Deputies, thanks to the farmers' votes, voted for Schacht, with the exception of the deputies from Bavaria, who were unanimously hostile.

This Dr. Schacht definitely provokes diametrically opposed reactions...

And what a surprise: in an unexpected burst of authority, President Ebert overrode all opposition and contrary opinions.

On December 22, 1923, three days before Christmas, Hjalmar Schacht was appointed president for life of the Reichsbank.

CHAPTER 4. THE NEGOTIATOR

Gentlemen! You are my collaborators today. I am aware that none of you have spoken out in favor of this situation. On the contrary, I am now taking over as President for life of the Reichsbank against your unanimous wish. I do not hold this against you, because in short, you know little about me. So, if you wish to remain at the Reichsbank and work loyally with me, you are welcome to do so. If not, I will gladly assist those of you who wish to find a position outside the Reichsbank. Please let me know your decision before tomorrow. Goodbye, gentlemen!

Thus, in the last days of 1923, I opened my first meeting of the Reichsbank board of directors as president for life of this prestigious institution. Half an hour after the meeting had ended, a delegation came to see me in the large, light-filled office of the Reichsbank President, which I had exchanged for my dark storeroom in the courtyard of the Ministry of Finance. All the members of the board of directors came to resign and stayed at the Reichsbank, promising me their loyalty.

The most powerful institution in the German economy was in my hands.

However, I still had a lot to do to stabilize the German economy and currency for good. And, despite my determination, I could not do it alone.

So I left for England on December 31, 1923. Despite the late hour of my arrival at Liverpool Station, the Governor of the Bank of England, Montagu Norman, whom I did not yet know but who was to become my great friend, was there on the platform to welcome me. The very next day, even though it was January 1, he received me in his magnificent medieval palace at the Bank of England on Threadneedle Street. I told him my plan:

- I need to get the German economy back on track. To do this, we need a stable currency that will allow us to restore economic exchange with the outside world. But I have a problem: I have no reserves, neither gold nor foreign currency. In short, I have no means!

- Are you coming to London for credit? I doubt that at this time, given the disorder of your country, you will find any," objected Norman.

- I'm not looking for a credit, Governor. I want to create a break. I will found a second monetary institute next to the Reichsbank, which will issue money based entirely on gold. This new bank, which I will call the Golddiskontbank, will have the task of financing Germany's foreign trade.

- And how do you intend to build up the capital of this bank, if you have no means?

- It will have a capital made up entirely of foreign currency. I'm making it my business to find a part of it in Germany, by scraping all the drawer bottoms. The rest I came here to find. The Golddiskontbank will have a capital in pounds sterling.

The next day, Montagu Norman received me again. On the strength of my name and reputation alone, he had decided that the Bank of England would agree to lend one hundred million pounds sterling to Germany, to enable the creation of the Golddiskontbank, at the particularly low rate of 5%, whereas I was expecting to pay 10%, which was the international market rate at the time. Dear Montagu Norman, he had given me a friendly price! Moreover, he had found the time to convince some of his London banker acquaintances to participate in the operation: the Golddiskontbank could start with a capital of half a billion!

I was not totally fooled by the quick agreement of the English in this matter. Certainly, I had inspired their confidence and they had been seduced by my plan. But it should also be pointed out that at that time they were on the outs with their French allies, whose scandalous behavior towards Germany they judged severely. Between the invasion of the Ruhr, the bullying of the German population and the intractable demand for payment of reparations, the French were trying to create the conditions for a new conflict. The British had therefore also been tempted by the idea of giving the froggies a kick in the ass by coming to Germany's aid.

In any case, within a few weeks, I had carried out the plan that I had meticulously prepared in the dusty gloom of the Ministry of Finance's maids' storeroom: I had stabilized the currency, brought inflation under control, restored some confidence in the authorities in charge of running the economy - in this case, me! - and set the conditions for a gradual recovery of the country's activity.

Of course, one should not deny the collateral damage that my policy had caused. Forced to repay the "emergency bonds" they had issued themselves, many German companies suffered heavy losses. As for the speculators and financiers, taken aback by my decision to prohibit all financing of their operations outside the official rates, many of them simply went out of business! But they only had themselves to blame.

The country was starting up again, and that alone was important. However, it was still hampered in its progress by the weight of its debt: the gigantic debt that had been imposed on it to pay war reparations was added to the formidable private debt of German companies to foreign banks, mainly English and American. Some of these creditors were intractable, such as the French, who used a delay in the delivery of telegraph poles as a pretext to invade the Ruhr. Others, such as the British and Americans, were more sympathetic.

But all of them, in fact, made serious errors of analysis in Germany's ability to pay, because the problem of debt is eminently complex to understand.

The debt, the repairs, the annual payments to be made in gold or in foreign currency... So many parameters to be considered with circumspection, even if you are not an economist.

Few realized to what extent the mechanism imagined by the Treaty of Versailles, if it had been applied, would have ruined the whole of Europe. Indeed, Germany had to pay, as war reparations, one hundred and thirty-two billion gold marks, at a rate of two to three billion gold marks per year. Sixty years of payments! Of course, these payments had to be made in foreign currency or in gold. Since Germany had no foreign currency, it had to obtain it through exports, and thus become a very strong exporting economic power again. In doing so, it had to compete with the countries to which it had to pay reparations, and gain foreign markets at their expense. The French, the British and the Americans demanded that Germany pay the reparations? Germany had to ruin French, British and American exporters to do so.

It was absurd and of course it never worked.

In reality, out of the one hundred and thirty-two billion originally planned, Germany paid a total of ten billion; and I must point out that this money came from loans, taken out by German companies in America or England, and not from the proceeds of our economic activity. We paid the Allies with their own money! And we stopped all payments as soon as I returned to power with Hitler in 1933.

My deepest feeling has always been that these reparations should not be paid. Of course, it was necessary to give the impression that Germany would not fail to do so, but without ever quite doing so. This is what I did in discussing the Young and Dawes plans for renegotiating reparations, and in creating the Bank for International Settlements: to make it appear that we were willing to pay, but never to pay more than token sums, or a few billion borrowed from our creditors themselves!

The question of the debt of countries is one that I was asked a lot about when, after the Second World War, I started a career as a consultant for many emerging countries. The thesis I have always defended is that when a debt becomes excessive, whether for a country or for an institution such as a bank or a company, then it constitutes a problem, not only for the debtor, but also for the creditors.

And creditors, just like the debtor, must be involved in solving this problem. I have often demonstrated this to my interlocutors in the following way.

Let's imagine a country indebted to the extent of the wealth it produces each year, that magic indicator that we call in economics the gross domestic product or GDP. Its debt ratio is therefore 100% of GDP.

This is a situation in which many countries may find themselves, at one time or another in their history.

Let's imagine now that it is estimated that this 100% debt ratio must fall to, say, 60%, in order to be sustainable for the economy.

Unless the creditors are asked to forgive part of this debt, the only solution is to force the country's population to pay higher taxes or to suffer a reduction in the wealth distributed by the state in order to repay the creditors a larger fraction of this excessive debt. Considering that this effort of austerity and rigor amounts to 2% of gdp, which is truly considerable, it is immediately clear that it will take twenty years of effort to reach the objective. And probably even more than twenty years: indeed, the restrictions imposed on the population will probably cause recessionary episodes during which the wealth produced, the GDP, will contract, which will make the foreseeable period of austerity even longer.

Creditors must participate in the solution of the problem they have created! There is no other way out when a debt becomes unsustainable!

Subjecting the population to twenty years or more of austerity and deprivation? Might as well say eternity? This is what the victors of the First World War sought to impose on the German population.

The idea was economically stupid and historically mortifying.

For, in the end, the result was Adolf Hitler.

Hjalmar Schacht, when he took up his post as President for life of the Reichsbank at Christmas time in 1923, could savor his success. He, the poor child from the suburbs of Hamburg, the son of an emigrant who did not know on which side of the Atlantic he should settle, the schoolboy in *shoddy* pants who defended his dignity with his fists in the *Gymnasium* courtyard, had been collecting titles of glory ever since he set out in life.

He shone in financial circles where he became rich.

He gained a foothold in politics through the party he founded just after the war.

He is the government's last resort to save the country from ruin.

He became the president of the Reichsbank; at 46 years old, he is now the most powerful man in the German economy and speaks on a par with a Thyssen, a Krupp or a Schröder, the greatest of German bosses.

But he still has a long way to go to make his mark on the country.

Hjalmar Schacht recalls the studies he made at the Sorbonne in France and the judgment he made on the state of the French economy: an economy lagging behind its immediate competitors, such as the United Kingdom or Germany.

He drew two conclusions, both of which turned out to be correct.

First of all, the burden of the French debt, in other words the reparations imposed after the 1870 war, was the cause of this delay in development, just as the burden of the reparations is today the ball and chain that is holding back the German economy.

Secondly, the French economic backwardness had indeed been transmitted to the French military apparatus, which had proved to be rather weak: the German armies, at the beginning of the war, had easily overpowered the French infantry divisions. If the balance of power was eventually redressed and tipped in favor of the Allies, the industrial power of the United Kingdom and, above all, the United States, received most of the credit. Only Uncle Sam's factories had allowed Germany to be finally defeated.

To repeat the French mistake of paying war reparations was therefore simply not an option for Hjalmar Schacht, in whose mind the rebirth of Germany was a sacred mission. Moreover, Schacht had struggled hard enough to restore a semblance of economic order in the country to let the payment of reparations upset the very fragile balance he had worked so hard to restore.

It was therefore necessary to find a way to negotiate payment terms with the creditors that would de facto cancel the obligation to pay.

In 1924, under pressure from the Germans and the Americans, the Dawes Commission, charged with renegotiating the war reparations owed by Germany, opened its work in Paris. For Schacht, this was an opportunity not to be missed! He was going to bamboozle the Allies who were bleeding his country dry!

Schacht, in his spare time, was a poet, so he had no difficulty in reaching an agreement with Charles Dawes, who was a musician, to ease the financial burden on Germany. And what a musician! Add to this the fact that the man in question was later a Nobel Peace Prize winner and Vice President of the United States, and you can see what an ally Hjalmar Schacht had up his sleeve: a partner as eclectic as himself.

Charles W. Dawes, the chairman of the commission that bears his name, composed the *Melody in A Major*, which became a favorite "encore" of violin legend Fritz Kreisler until his death in the 1960s, and which singing star Elton John, and others before him, turned into the world-famous standard *It's all in the game*: a lovely, wistful melody about tears falling and lovers meeting again. In the ranking of the one hundred most beautiful songs ever written, it occupies the thirty-fifth place.

But Charles Dawes was primarily a lawyer and financier. His eclectic background also led him to a military stint as a brigadier general in the U.S. Army during World War I. Later, like General Sherman after World War II, he was charged by U.S. President Calvin Coolidge with preventing the collapse of the European economy. Like Hjalmar Schacht, Charles Dawes was convinced that the implementation of the war reparations payment plan imposed on Germany would lead to the economic collapse of Europe. And since Europe was the number one customer for American industry, this amateur musician and professional financier did not want that to happen.

When Dawes opened the work of the Allied Reparations Commission in Paris, it was with open opposition from the French, who remained firm in their diktat: no concessions should be made to Germany. Germany had lost the war, it had to pay! Period.

Hjalmar Schacht, the new president of the Reichsbank, was "summoned" to appear before the Dawes Commission in January 1924, like a defendant before a court.

Germany does not pay?

Why?

By what right?

Please explain yourself, *Doktor* Schacht!

Schacht was seated like a satrap in ancient Persia, at the end of the table facing all the delegates. But one does not impress the great Hjalmar Schacht with such poor expedients. The *Herr Doktor* set out his views with vigor and clarity. He had only been head of the Reichsbank for a few weeks, but already he could claim monetary stabilization as his achievement, and this was achieved with Germany's own resources. He therefore commands the respect of the members of the Dawes Commission, even when he exposes what tragic risks, from his point of view, the payment of reparations would run for the entire European economy.

We listen to him. The commission heard Schacht on several occasions. Schacht's strength of conviction was such that even the French representative seemed to be shaken from time to time.

Schacht was an outstanding negotiator and eventually won the game.

If one takes stock of who won and who lost, the Dawes plan was indeed a great success for Schacht. The payment of reparations was rescheduled, the debt was reduced and now only had to be repaid over 36 years instead of 60, and above all, the plan imposed a reorganization of the Reichsbank that gave the institution total independence from political power. It can therefore be said that the central banks of today, if they have gained their independence from governments, owe it in large part to Hjalmar Schacht, Hitler's banker!

Satisfied with himself, the new president of the Reichsbank also took advantage of his stay in Paris to make the rounds of the top French politicians: he was received by the President of the Republic, Alexandre Millerand, by the Minister of Foreign Affairs and by the Governor of the Bank of France. But these incorrigible Frenchmen sometimes tried to humiliate the arrogant German, this loser of the war who came to give them lessons in economics! In the antechamber of Raymond Poincaré, the President of the Council, he was kept waiting.

Five minutes.

Ten minutes.

Then more.

Schacht becomes impatient, his fingers drum on the arm of the chair, his feet are animated by spasmodic movements. "Who do we think we are dealing with?" he grumbles.

He stands up, calls out to the bailiff:

- Dear friend, you will advise the President of the Council that I cannot wait any longer!

And Schacht, the loser of the war, turns on his heels and strides away. As he left the ministry, the bailiff caught up with him.

- Doctor Schacht! Dr. Schacht! Mr. President of the Council will see you immediately!

Schacht was inwardly jubilant. He majestically went up the stairs of the ministry to return to the antechamber, the bailiff hanging on his heels like a little dog in tow of his master. Raymond Poincaré, red with anger and confusion, was on the threshold of his office waiting for the German. The latter slowly advances, dominating the Frenchman with his high stature. He holds out his hand for a slightly condescending *shake-hands.* How triumphant the great Hjalmar Schacht was, shaking hands with the head of the French government for a long time!

So, his whole person seems to be saying, who is the loser now?

After the Dawes Plan, Schacht was no longer just the most powerful man in the economy in Germany. In the face of the still weak and wavering power of the Weimar Republic, he, Schacht, had become the president for life of the Reichsbank, the most powerful man in Germany. The Dawes Plan did include a foreign representative, Seymour Parker Gilbert, who was responsible for ensuring that the reparations were paid, as well as a supervisory board: composed of seven Germans and seven foreigners, it was theoretically responsible for controlling the actions of the Reichsbank president, who was decidedly too anxious to have his hands free of all constraints. In the six years of its existence, the supervisory board never voted against any of his decisions, even when he decided to cut off all credit to the economy during a crisis that threatened his great work, monetary stabilization.

And above all, Schacht never paid a penny more in reparations! All that was paid during this period, i.e., a few billion gold marks, was duly borrowed, especially from American banks. Paying creditors with their own money: excellent gangster films have been made on this theme. Well, the script was written by *Herr Doktor* Hjalmar Schacht!

But of course, as the years went by, the Allies eventually realized the maneuver.

They arrive at this conclusion: Germany does not pay its obligations with money from its exports, but with money borrowed from themselves! This is a breach of the Treaty of Versailles; a serious problem to be solved!

Finding the solution is another matter...

Everyone knows that to bury a problem and avoid tackling it head-on, all you have to do is create a commission. All governments, including today's, use and abuse this delaying tactic which consists in pretending to tackle a problem head-on. The ins and outs of the issue are discussed at length among very learned people in good company, comfortably seated in a hushed meeting room, hoping that time and oblivion will serve as a substitute for the courage to make the necessary decisions. As a French politician of the 1950s, Henri Queuille, the former President of the Council, said with finesse, whose rigorously non-existent political work is totally forgotten today: "There is no problem that an absence of solution cannot, in the long run, contribute to solving."

In February 1929, the war reparations negotiating commission reopened at the George V Hotel in the Champs-Élysées district. Hjalmar Schacht returned to Paris. Among the participants in the commission, American bankers were represented by Jack Pierpont Morgan Jr, the eldest son of John Pierpont Morgan, founder of the great Morgan Bank, a major player in 20th century finance and still active today.

The chairman of the commission is the American Owen D. Young.

Was Charles Dawes a musician? Young was not, but he probably helped Dawes cultivate the popularity of his *Melody in A major*, for he was the founder of the famous radio station RCA - Radio Corporation America - which later became a gigantic American television empire. Young was also, for almost twenty years, the president of the giant American group General Electric. He also ran for the U.S. presidential election in 1932, but failed to win the Democratic Party nomination and rallied behind Franklin Roosevelt, who was elected to the highest office.

Owen Young, who participated in the Dawes Commission, wanted to change tactics from the previous round of negotiations, which had not produced any convincing results. In his opinion, it was pointless to impose again on Germany an amount of reparations that it could not pay. It would be better to ask the Germans for measurable and objective economic data, to determine how much they can pay, according to a rigorous and econometric approach, and then try to build a payment schedule on this basis.

Schacht immediately adapted to this tactic.

The commission members want to know how much Germany wants to pay?

Good! He will provide them with numbers! Hundreds of numbers! Thousands and thousands of numbers that multiply again and again, like wheat in the summer wind.

Schacht had the Reichsbank prepare volumes and volumes of documentation. A considerable mass of figures, tables, graphs, notes, studies, statistics, in short, tens of thousands of pages to read and integrate! Hjalmar Schacht invented a strategy that would meet with great success: above all, never refuse to provide information. On the contrary, provide information, more information, always more information, in short, drown your interlocutors under a deluge of data, figures, concepts, documents, some useful, others, many others, a lot of others, perfectly useless... and bet on discouragement, lassitude, the propensity of the human mind to go for the fastest, simplest and least conflicting solution The bet is usually a winner every time.

Speaking of weariness... After a few weeks of these technical discussions about endless numbers, Schacht once again came out the winner of the confrontation: J. P. Morgan, Jr, the American representative, could no longer stand it. He left for the Mediterranean to rest on his yacht.

End of the story.

Schacht wins the fight by K.O.

There was a new rescheduling and a reduction of the debt - Germany committed itself to paying thirty-four billion reichsmarks over fifty-nine years, i.e. until 1988 - but with no more result than during the Dawes Plan: Germany would only ever pay with borrowed money, and for amounts much lower than the planned annuities. The payments ceased definitively when Hitler came to power, with the return of Schacht as president of the Reichsbank.

But Hjalmar Schacht, as an aesthete, wanted the Young Commission to end its work in an elegant way: with delicate subtlety, he cooked up a final trick.

- You see, Mr. Young," he once said, "the main problem with these repairs is that it's impossible to identify who is paying for what, and how they are paying for it. The financial flows go through various channels that are very complex to analyze. In these conditions, reconstructing payment amounts is a challenge.

- Certainly, *Herr Doktor* Schacht, answers Young. The impressive volume of documentation that you have produced for us demonstrates the relevance of your point of view. But what solution do you propose?

- A new monetary institute should be created. I have experience of such a creation with the Golddiskontbank. Unlike the Golddiskontbank, this new kind of monetary institute would have to be supranational. It would keep the accounts of the central banks of the whole world and would also serve as a channel for the war reparations that we would be able to pay. This is a modern and efficient solution!

- The idea sounds attractive," agrees Owen Young. It would also have the advantage of leaving a tangible record of our commission's work; a mark in history, so to speak... Where do you think this institute could be established?

- I leave that to the discretion of the commission," Schacht replied. I had thought of Brussels, but since Belgium is on the side of the Allies, the German people would probably appreciate it more if the institute were located in a neutral country. Switzerland, for example...

In 1930, the Bank for International Settlements (BIS) was inaugurated in Basel, Switzerland.

The civil servants who work in this esteemed institution owe their jobs to the devil's banker, Hjalmar Schacht. But do they realize that the creation of the BIS was nothing more than a gigantic scam? For if Schacht, in suggesting the creation of this institute, was ostensibly showing an obvious willingness to pay, this demiurge of communication had the very firm intention of continuing as before, that is to say, to compete for every pfennig that would leave the country. It was certainly not his intention to bleed the German economy to pay the reparations for a war that had ended ten years earlier.

Bravo ! Masterfully played! Respect to Hjalmar Schacht, master negotiator... And king of the swindlers!

Eighty years have passed since BIS opened its doors. Some ironic commentators sometimes say that the scam continues. The Bank for International Settlements is home to the so-called "Basel" committees that set standards for banks to ensure global financial stability. These standards were in place at the onset of the 2008 financial crisis, which they were dramatically unable to stop. It will probably take 20 years for the global economy to recover, if it ever does.

This is a demoralizing observation, because the probability that Schacht will rise from his grave to imagine solutions to end this 21st century crisis is, alas, infinitesimal...

Chapter 5. The Nazi

I resigned from the presidency of the Reichsbank on March 7, 1930.

The chancellery was then occupied by Heinrich Brüning, a centrist, honest enough man, but so irresolute and ineffective in his policies that it plunged the country into a new crisis almost as serious as that of hyperinflation. The social consequences were even more dramatic. Brüning was not entirely to blame: in October 1929, the collapse of the Wall Street stock exchange had plunged the world into a terrible recession, and poor Brüning was ill-equipped to deal with an event of this magnitude in our troubled Germany.

The great American writer Mark Twain said it best: "October is a particularly dangerous month to play the stock market. But there are others: November, December, January, February..."

And these months passed with an accumulation of calamities for Germany caught in the grip of the world crisis, with a Brüning at its head, unable to govern.

Brüning liked to play the normal man, an average middle-class man from an average province, with an average political career in an average party, with average ideas and the ability to make strong decisions, which were also hopelessly average. In other words, he was not the right man for the job. During his term of office, his erratic and disordered decisions caused far more harm than good. In addition to aggravating the crisis rather than providing a solution, the resulting social disorder encouraged the rise of extremes on both the right and the left, making the country ungovernable.

In any case ungovernable by him.

For my part, I sensed that even more serious events were about to occur in the economy. My fears were on the side of the banking system. It seemed obvious to me that the growth of foreign debts would, at some point, result in bank failures. The Reichsbank, lacking the institutional powers and even the financial means - especially the necessary foreign currency resources - was not in a position to prevent this.

My warnings to the Brüning government went unheeded. If things had not been so dramatic, I would have been almost amused: Brüning claimed to have some competence in economics - he had been Finance Minister - but his blindness to the warning signs was quite astounding.

Brüning implemented a very strange economic policy. While unemployment was tragically increasing day by day, he set out to restore the state's accounts. The timing, as the Americans say, was most unfortunate. Of course, it would have been necessary to do the opposite, to relaunch investments, to create activities, but this was something that Brüning, the normal, average Brüning, did not understand. Instead, he embarked on a deflationary policy: adding deflation to recession was his recipe for restoring the balance of public finances... To hear him explain why was a stunning experience!

I could have lived with his economic policy, or even tried, as head of the Reichsbank, to limit its harmful effects in order to try to save what could be saved in the country.

But the day came when Brüning was unable to show any character in the face of the demands of the European members of the Allied camp, France, Belgium and the United Kingdom; the Americans were still better disposed towards us. These European countries were questioning what I had negotiated so hard, and obtained, in the Young Plan. I decided that the measure was full. Brüning, all imbued with his normality and mediocrity, did not feel the strength to resist external injunctions? To force his nature, I put my resignation on the line: I had negotiated foot to foot with the Young Commission to preserve Germany's interests, so it was out of the question for me that the German government would not support me, Hjalmar Schacht, its official representative. But it was a waste of time: Brüning was too normal, too average and therefore too soft to not give in to the Europeans.

I could have been stubborn and stayed on as head of the Reichsbank, but I didn't belong with those people anymore. I might as well have left them to face their responsibilities. And who knows? Maybe they were right and I was wrong? The future would show...

On March 7, 1930, Field Marshal Hindenburg, the head of state, accepted my resignation from the presidency of the Reichsbank, expressly asking me not to make public the reasons for my departure. I complied with his request and remained discreet about my disagreements with the government: my aim was obviously not to add disorder to disorder.

The following years proved how right I was.

The banking crisis I had feared was triggered in the spring of 1931. An Austrian bank, the Kreditanstalt, failed. Germany should not have been affected by this bankruptcy, but since in the confused minds of Americans the two countries were similar, the American banks violently withdrew their capital from our institutions, making it almost impossible to finance their business. Without American credits, the economy I had restarted came to a standstill. The Reichsbank then had to deplete its foreign exchange reserves to prevent the Reichsmark from collapsing; it succeeded acrobatically, but the result was a highly weakened German banking system and the Reichsbank's ability to act became non-existent.

We were still alive, but on the edge of the precipice, praying that the ground would not give way under our feet.

A second event brought the country into crisis.

Throughout the world, for as long as finance has existed, knights of industry, high-flying swindlers and dubious businessmen have occupied the front pages of the news. They build empires on mountains of debt, compromise politicians by their prevarication, frequent the gotha and high society by offering sumptuous receptions, and cultivate their image with the public thanks to their charm and aplomb. One need only read the business pages of newspapers to identify these nefarious characters who haunt all eras; they usually end up leaving the limelight with a landscape of disaster behind them.

We had such a bandit in Germany in the suit of a respectable businessman: Carl Lahusen was the boss of the largest textile company in northern Germany, the Nordwolle Group of Bremen. He had built it up through an ingenious, but perfectly illegal, system of banking cavalry, which collapsed with the bankruptcy of the Austrian Kreditanstalt, of which the Nordwolle Group was one of the first clients. Nordwolle was then declared bankrupt. My former bank, the Danat Bank, which I managed before I became president of the Reichsbank, was involved with Nordwolle to the tune of fifty million Reichsmarks. It too went bankrupt, causing a nationwide bank run, a rush of savers to withdraw their money from their accounts in cash. It was then July 13. In the days that followed, terribly weakened by these withdrawals and despite the closure of the counters of all the banks in the country for two days, another establishment, the Dresdner Bank, the first German bank, the same one where I had known my glorious beginnings in finance, declared itself bankrupt. Then came Deutsche Bank and Kommerzbank, which were saved by the state in extremis.

Sometimes jealous of the achievements of men, the gods punish them by mercilessly destroying their greatest masterpieces...

The gods had been particularly severe with me.

Fate had stretched out its vengeful arm over everything I had built up since my youth through hard work: the Danat Bank was dead, the Dresdner Bank was dead, the Reichsbank was bloodless, the German economy was once again at the bottom of the abyss, and more than six million unemployed people were running the streets in search of sustenance, ready to follow a providential guide who would put them out of their misery.

When I think back to that animal Brüning, that normal man, I am stunned! He again showed an understanding of the situation that defied comprehension by choosing this moment to accentuate his deflationary policy, all preoccupied as he was with his sole objective: at all costs, to achieve a balance in public finances! He probably wanted the country to die, but in good health...

Fortunately, Hindenburg finally dismissed Brüning, whom the people had nicknamed "the chancellor of hunger". It was May 1932. Too late; the damage was done.

For my part, I had witnessed this collapse with my heart clenched by so much incompetence that caused so much distress. Choosing the right people to govern is really of crucial importance for the running of a country, especially in times of crisis. The Germans realized this and the lesson of the "normal man" was extraordinarily expensive.

The parliamentary elections of September 1930 had led to one hundred and seven elected members of a new party, the NSDAP, Nationalsozialistische Deutsche Arbeiterpartei, otherwise known as the Nazi Party, being elected to the House of Representatives, the Reichstag. Its leader was an Austrian, a certain Adolf Hitler, whose writings I had read: a book entitled Mein Kampf, *of rather mediocre literary quality. The economic program of this individual was not very precise; obviously, it had yet to be defined. I wondered about Hitler's chances of coming to power one day, especially since he was not German; he would not officially obtain citizenship until February 1932. I was, I confess, rather circumspect. I met Adolf Hitler incidentally a few times, at the home of a mutual acquaintance, Hermann Göring, also a member of the Nazi party. I liked the man moderately. However, his energy, his oratorical qualities and his determination were striking.*

Determination was what brought us together. I was not seduced by Hitler, but the conviction grew in me that this man, correctly advised, skilfully guided, could be an asset in the new renaissance of Germany, the renaissance of which I had been the architect as President of the Reichsbank and which others, by their carelessness, had managed to euthanize.

However, I, Hjalmar Schacht, had nothing to do with Adolf Hitler's rise to power!

Contrary to the odious accusations I have been accused of, I have never sought to favour him!

After his departure from the Reichsbank, Schacht disappeared from public life for a while. A few years earlier, he had acquired a vast estate in Gühlen, not far from Berlin; the great financier devoted his time to raising pigs, running his brickworks and organizing hunts for his acquaintances in the few remaining forests around his property: most of the trees had in fact been cut down to make telegraph poles, which were to be delivered to the Allies as part of the war reparations. Schacht was definitely being pursued by these damned repairs!

Hjalmar Schacht did not leave public life altogether: lecture tours in Europe and the United States allowed him to meet prominent political figures, including the American President Herbert Hoover. He mingled with Berlin's social life, dining with his former business contacts.

Until January 5, 1931.

That evening, Hjalmar Schacht and his wife were invited to the Göring home. In addition to Hermann Göring and his wife, the couple Goebbels and the industrialist Fritz Thyssen were there: the army with Göring, propaganda with Goebbels and capital with Thyssen surrounded Schacht the financier.

The four pillars of the future Nazi regime are united.

Then Adolf Hitler enters.

No wonder: Hitler is at home here. Hermann Göring, the Luftwaffe hero of World War I, and Joseph Goebbels, the journalist who became the master of the Hitler press, were early Nazis. Both joined the party in 1922; Göring immediately attached himself to Hitler's side, while Goebbels, initially, was rather close to the Strasser brothers, Otto and Gregor, with whom Hitler was competing for the leadership of the Nazi movement. But Goebbels later rallied to Hitler and is now part of the first circle of loyalists.

The presence of Fritz Thyssen is also natural: as early as 1923, this very rich industrialist sympathized with the Nazi party, to the point of being one of its first donors. The hundred thousand gold marks that Thyssen gave to Hitler in 1923 allowed the Nazi leader to finance his attempted coup in Munich. Later, in 1930, Thyssen personally bought, together with other German fortunes, the Munich building, the *Braune Haus* ("Brown House"), which became the headquarters of the Nazi party; Thyssen renovated it entirely at his own expense. The fate of Nazi Fritz Thyssen was curious, because this loyal supporter of Hitler was not anti-Semitic and believed rather in the cohabitation of religions and peoples. Moreover, because he was imbued with a strong personal ethic, Thyssen wanted to live in accordance with this personal faith of respect for a religion that was hated by his fellow students. This kind of schizophrenia was difficult to assume in the heart of the Third Reich. The "Kristallnacht" of November 9, 1938, during which Jewish stores were devastated throughout Germany, while Jewish families were victims of violent pogroms everywhere, had a revelatory effect on Fritz Thyssen: he fled to Switzerland, then to France. Hitler confiscated all his assets in Germany. Two years later, Thyssen took refuge in Nice. At the end of 1940, the Vichy police arrested him and handed him over to the Gestapo on December 26. Like Schacht a few years later, he was one of Hitler's "special" prisoners, those who spent long periods of time in the concentration camps, benefiting from a special regime that gave them some chance of survival.

Schacht and Thyssen, the representatives of big business, survived the Nazi adventure.

The three other guests at the dinner, Göring, Goebbels and Hitler himself, would lose their lives, all by suicide. A testimony, perhaps, to the immemorial superiority of the power of money over the power of politics, even in times of extreme violence...

In any case, on this Monday evening of January 5, 1931, in the icy Berlin night, five men, two future prisoners and three future suicides, are gathered together to taste in all urbanity the pea soup with bacon that constitutes the frugal supper offered by *Frau* Göring, this blond Swedish sylph who languidly drags her fragile health from armchair to sofa.

Adolf Hitler, barely touching his plate, was not a man who flaunted wealth and power like Hjalmar Schacht. He is dressed in a simple brown jacket, as sober as Schacht's traditional dark suit. No, like Schacht, he did not need any external signs to impress those around him.

All he has to do is talk.

And Hitler speaks.

Schacht was impressed by the resolution of the Nazi leader and by the feeling of absolute confidence that he exuded. Goebbels and Göring only listened, without saying a word, and only nodded their approval of Hitler's words. Thyssen intervened, but very briefly, and only when Hitler began to address financial issues.

Schacht was attentive to the Nazi leader's proposals; they contained nothing unreasonable, they were expressed with measure and did not present economic nonsense, as Schacht might have feared. Hitler did not give a propaganda speech, but calmly, pedagogically, and with an almost palpable determination, explained what he would do to straighten out Germany if he were called to power.

Schacht was not really convinced by Adolf Hitler's ideas. The Nazi leader explained that he wanted to put an end to the endemic unemployment that was undermining German society - six million people were unemployed at the time - by launching major infrastructure and industrial renovation programs.

Either.

In terms of principles, it's a pretty good idea.

But this is not enough.

For Hitler had few ideas about how to proceed. He did not measure the risks to monetary equilibrium that a stimulus policy presented: the return of inflation would mean the ruin of all these fine projects. Similarly, Hitler had no opinion on how to finance his investment plan.

Borrow?

But to whom?

To the Germans themselves, through a large national subscription?

With six million people unemployed in the country, Hjalmar Schacht knew that every German family had at least one unemployed person, either in the family itself or among its relatives. The entire population suffered from this unemployment and restricted its consumption; in addition, the savings of German households had been eroded by successive financial crises. Consequently, there is little hope of mobilizing Germany's own resources.

Borrowing from the Americans and the British?

They had helped Germany in the past, especially when Schacht was in charge. The presence of the German big money man at the head of the Reichsbank inspired them with confidence. Today, that confidence has disappeared: foreign banks are desperate to recover their capital. To reverse this trend and bring back American investors, we need a man who will restore this confidence. Hitler was certainly not that man, and the economists he had in his party, such as Walther Funk, a journalist of little talent, or Gottfried Feder, that compulsive anti-Semite, had no audience outside the narrow circle of the National Socialist Party.

No, it would take a real economist, of international stature, who could steer the Nazi program in the right direction...

- So, *Doktor* Schacht, what do you think?" asks Adolf Hitler.

- *Herr* Hitler, your program is attractive, but there are many prerequisites to be met. For example...

- *Gut!"* cuts in Hitler. You're probably right! After all, you are the specialist. But I take note that you agree with my proposals.

- But, *Herr* Hitler," Schacht tries to say, "there is a problem of means...

- You are right again, *Doktor* Schacht!" interrupts Hitler. The means! The resources! The financing! It is imperative that we find the necessary means, first to come to power, then to implement our program. Fritz who is here will help us," adds Hitler, pointing to Fritz Thyssen. In addition, the party is registering new memberships every day. We will be the leading political force in Germany in the next elections. But we must do more, faster and stronger. The recovery of the German nation depends on it! You can play a big role, Dr. Schacht!

- Certainly, *Herr* Hitler, but all this is a bit premature and...

- *Jawohl, Doktor* Schacht! We will see the details later! In the meantime, I suggest that we do this...

And Hitler continued his speech, with Göring and Goebbels nodding silently from time to time in approval.

This other trait of the Nazi leader strikes Hjalmar Schacht: a discussion with Hitler consists of 95% monologue and 5% dialogue. But it doesn't matter: at the end of the night's discussions, Schacht feels the conviction germinate in him that Hitler, correctly accompanied and oriented, can become the leader the country needs to get out of the quicksand in which it is drowning a little more each day.

At the bottom of the Göring building, with their feet in the snow of that January night, Hitler and Schacht shook hands. Schacht greeted Fritz Thyssen and the Goebbels, then helped his wife into the car and drove back to his hotel. It was five o'clock in the morning; since leaving the Reichsbank, Schacht had no driver, and it was too late to return to his estate in Gühlen, some 60 kilometers away. It would be unwise to drive that far in the icy night on icy roads.

As he enters the brightly lit lobby of the Adlon Hotel, Hjalmar Schacht, who has been silent since they left the Göring apartment, is interrupted in his thoughts by his wife.

"You know, Hjalmar, you have to help him! This Hitler is the man we need. I have met many great leaders with you; I have never felt such magnetism in any of them. Including Hoover, the American!"

Schacht does not answer anything.

In the years that followed, Louise, the pretty ice skater he had married two decades earlier and who became, through pregnancies and gala dinners, a somewhat thick woman, would become an enthusiastic Nazi muse and fierce Adolf Hitler worshipper.

Not Hjalmar Schacht, whose mode of operation is centered on reason, not on affect.

But this time, he agrees with his wife.

This Hitler can be a solution.

However, he had some bizarre, not to say disturbing, aspects, such as his hostile feelings towards Jews or Slavic populations. He did not hide this: he openly expressed these questionable opinions in his book *Mein Kampf*. But with a Schacht at his side, this agitator with undeniable energy and obvious determination could put an end to these inconsistent leaders whose weakness was leading the country to bankruptcy...

It's decided.

He will help Hitler!

He, Hjalmar Schacht, will be the linchpin of Adolf Hitler's accession to the chancellery, and thus he will save the nation from the ruin that threatens it once again!

A strange phenomenon of denial struck Hjalmar Schacht about his responsibility and his role in the arcanes of Hitler's power.

For half a dozen years after the Second World War, he was dragged from court to court, from court to prison, in order to be denazified. He never admitted that Adolf Hitler owed his accession to the post of chancellor to him. He never conceded that the consolidation of Nazi power was his doing. Never did he agree that the German army owed its war power to him.

"I never said a single word or wrote a single line to help Hitler come to power!"

This leitmotif was Hjalmar Schacht's immutable line of defense. He used a well-known and often effective strategy: deny, always deny, deny against the evidence, deny even when evidence to the contrary is produced, right there in front of you. Deny and deny again.

And always repeat the same thing.

"I never said a single word or wrote a single line to help Hitler come to power!"

Lie. Huge lie!

Indeed, the powerful financier will devote himself to the Hitler cause. Moreover, he will try to gather around him the great German capital so that the Nazi party reaches the power.

In the weeks following this dinner, Hjalmar Schacht intervened with the politicians with whom he was in contact, and even with Chancellor Brüning, whom he had known for more than twenty years, in order to get the National Socialists into the government. It was a waste of time; governing with extremists, for Brüning the "normal man", was simply not an option. Of course, these were right-wing extremists; left-wing extremists, i.e. communists, frightened him even more. But even so, Brüning was not yet so desperate, nor was his popularity so destroyed, that this "normal man" and humanist was forced to accept that fanatical extremists share power.

Brüning refused.

After all, in his eyes, the NSDAP, even if it constituted the second largest force in the Reichstag with its 107 deputies, was only ever a formation freshly and very provisionally consecrated by the ballot box. For years, the Nazis had been nothing more than a small group of violent agitators who had failed to make their mark on the German political scene. The recent past of these troublemakers gave hope that they might disappear or fade away.

Brüning was referring to the past few years in which the Nazi party had not achieved any real electoral success. In the 1924 elections, the NSDAP had won two million votes and twenty-four seats. But the election took place six months after the failed putsch attempt in Munich; the insurrection had given the Nazis a lot of publicity, hence their unexpected electoral success. A few months after this initial success, new parliamentary elections were held; this time the Nazis were crushed. This time the Nazis were crushed. They received only 900,000 votes. In the following elections, in 1928, they were no more successful: 800,000 votes.

The same decline in popularity of the Nazi party was bound to happen again at some point, Brüning thought.

The Chancellor would not admit it, but those years were over.

In the September 1930 elections, the National Socialist Party won nearly six and a half million votes and one hundred and seven deputies. The Nazis then constituted the second largest parliamentary group in the Reichstag, behind the traditional right. Adolf Hitler became a man whose words counted in the political debate; he was no longer the aggressive and voluble leader of a small group of enlightened extremists, but a politician with the wind in his sails and in whom the Germans, desperate for their leaders unable to stem the crisis, began to believe.

The dinner at the Göring's house reinforces this conviction in Hjalmar Schacht.

Chancellor Brüning was never won over to this view: for once, he resisted Schacht's recommendations when Schacht came to him to intercede for even a minimal participation of the Nazis in his government.

He refused outright.

But Schacht did not admit defeat. He had to persevere.

Despite the failure of his attempts to transform the Nazi party into a formation capable of joining the government, Hjalmar Schacht continued to cultivate his contacts with those close to Hitler. He had several meetings with Gottfried Feder, a Nazi deputy, who presented himself as an economist. Feder, a self-taught man, inspired Hitler to write many of his theories on the evils of "Jewish finance". In *Mein Kampf*, Hitler quotes Feder several times. Both share the same hatred of the Jews; the only difference is that Feder tries to give a scientific basis to this primal and visceral hatred. The book he wrote in 1934, *Die Juden*, is particularly detestable in this respect.

Schacht was edified: no, really, if the Nazis ever governed, it was imperative that economic policy be entrusted to him and to no one else. And especially not to this Feder with whom Hitler seemed to be infatuated. It is clear that Hitler must come to power, but with him, Hjalmar Schacht; otherwise the country is heading for disaster.

A little more patience.

In May 1932, his unpopularity was such that Chancellor Brüning was dismissed by Marshal Hindenburg. Despite a new intervention by Schacht in favour of Hitler, the old head of state entrusted the chancellorship to Franz von Papen, a right-wing demagogue, whose first move was to dissolve the Reichstag in order to provoke new elections and try to obtain a favourable majority in parliament.

Bad inspiration: on July 31, the Nazi party won more than thirteen and a half million votes. It was now the leading political force in Germany and had 230 deputies in the Reichstag, twice as many as before. However, Hindenburg again refused to draw the consequences. The old marshal was attached to traditional Prussian values; governing with this rough-hewn Austrian, Hitler, who had nothing of a democrat and everything of a dictator, was simply not an option.

He kept Franz von Papen in the chancellery.

A strange gun, this Franz von Papen!

Twisted, manipulative, not hesitating to betray his friends and rally his enemies, this aristocrat is as fervent a Catholic outwardly as he is intrinsically devoid of any Christian values. Papen embraced in his youth a career where his taste for plotting, his aptitude for lying and his capacity for dissimulation usually work wonders: espionage. As a young officer, he entered the diplomatic service: he was appointed military attaché to the German embassy in Mexico City, then in Washington, from which he was expelled manu militari in 1915, even though the United States was not yet at war. The young spy had not been discreet: he had engaged in sabotage activities on American territory and Uncle Sam's police, whose sense of humor was as lacking at the time as it is today, had only moderately enjoyed the joke. Papen was sent back to his home country and assigned to Madrid, then seconded to the Turkish Army Staff, which he followed in its conquest of the Middle East. His aptitude for plotting and dubious maneuvers was then expressed in the career of a politician that he began after the First World War, and which led him to the German Chancellery. He held the position of chancellor for six months. After leaving office, he accepted ambassadorial posts in Vienna and then in Turkey, where, during the Second World War, he recalled his youth as a master spy: Papen was the handler for Elyesa Baza, alias "Cicero", the valet who spied on the British ambassador in Istanbul and passed on Allied diplomatic secrets to Germany. Finally, along with Schacht, Papen was one of the defendants at the Nuremberg trial and, like Schacht, he was acquitted, thanks in particular to the testimony of Cardinal Roncalli, the future Pope John XXIII.

This is the extraordinary journey, in an extraordinary period, of an extraordinary character, an almost caricatured archetype of the politician who is used to all kinds of treachery and compromise.

After the elections of July 31, 1932, which established the Nazis as the leading political force in Germany, Papen managed to convince Hindenburg not to entrust the chancellorship to Hitler. For him, it was better to take the risk of dissolving the Chamber once again and to bet on a fall of these extremists. In the meantime, Papen remained in the German chancellor's chair.

The country is waiting for a real outcome that will bring hope. Everyone is holding their breath for the November elections: let's hope that this new dissolution, the second in a few months, will finally bring a solution!

Disappointed hope.

On November 6, 1932, the elections took place in an atmosphere of resignation. The Nazi party saw its audience erode: it went from thirteen million seven hundred thousand votes to eleven million seven hundred thousand votes, a drop from 37 to 33% of the country's voters. But the erosion is not enough. In losing two million votes and thirty-four seats in the Reichstag, the NSDAP nevertheless remained the leading party in Germany.

This electoral manoeuvre was again a bad inspiration. Brüning, whose normality contrasted with the dark and dubious personality of his successor, had missed everything. In the autumn of 1932, Franz von Papen, the unscrupulous politician, was going down the same path. What is this fatality that strikes Germany?

Hindenburg understands that he will not achieve anything with Papen who has just lost two legislative elections in less than four months. He had to be replaced.

But above all, don't tell him about Hitler! The old Prussian does not want him at any price!

Franz von Papen was ousted from the chancellery in favor of his close enemy, General Kurt von Schleicher.

The new chancellor tried to form a government with a few Nazis, but without Hitler, whom he rightly feared wanted to install a dictatorship. Schleicher obtained the appointment of Gregor Strasser, Hitler's former rival for the leadership of the National Socialist Party, as Vice-Chancellor. Schleicher also thought he had the confidence of Ernst Röhm, the supreme leader of the SA, the *Sturmabteilungen*, the paramilitary organization of the Nazi party. Thus, he believed that he could muzzle Nazi attempts to overthrow his government.

In this pre-insurrection atmosphere, with Nazi troops, SS and SA, reigning terror in the country, Papen is in his element; turning his coat again, he now plots to overthrow Kurt von Schleicher and bring Hitler to power. Hindenburg, sick and tired, gave in under pressure and signed Adolf Hitler's nomination. He was tired of resisting the pressure that was mounting. After all, very respectable personalities intervened with him in favor of Hitler:

Hjalmar Schacht, for example, or Thyssen, or Krupp. People whose opinion carried weight. People in whom he trusted. Great German patriots.

So why not try Hitler?

Papen, Schacht and all those who campaigned for Adolf Hitler finally won the decision. The Nazi leader was received by Hindenburg, who announced the resignation of the government and told him that he was going to hand over power to him.

The Schleicher government lasted only eight weeks.

On January 30, 1933, Hitler was officially installed as Chancellor of Germany.

A few weeks after taking power, the Nazis set fire to the Reichstag, the German parliament. The aim of the operation orchestrated by Göring and Goebbels was to make the Nazi party appear as the savior of the nation threatened by the danger posed by left-wing extremists. A scapegoat was designated as the arsonist; he was a young unemployed man of Dutch origin, Marinus van der Lubbe. He presented himself as a communist. He was sentenced to death and beheaded, but that was no longer important. The main thing was to alert the population to the Red Scare and to reinforce the image of Hitler as the savior of the country.

The plan is successful, but not as successful as its proponents had hoped.

In March 1933, new parliamentary elections, the third in less than a year, gave the Nazi party seventeen million three hundred thousand votes and 43.9% of the vote. The Nazis had never obtained an absolute majority in popular elections in Germany, but it did not matter, because two days after his enthronement, the new parliament voted Hitler full powers.

The dictatorship can begin.

A year and a half later, during the "Night of the Long Knives", from June 29 to 30, 1934, Adolf Hitler eliminated all those who competed with him for power during the crucial few weeks that led to his appointment as chancellor.

Schleicher is shot in his house with his wife.

Gregor Strasser, Hitler's rival in the Nazi party who had accepted the post of vice-chancellor in the Schleicher government, was arrested and taken to the Gestapo jails in Berlin, where he was executed with a bullet in the back of his neck.

Ernst Röhm, who had supported Schleicher, was captured in the midst of a homosexual orgy with very young ephebes belonging to the SA. He suffered the same fatal fate; Röhm was assassinated after a few days of hesitation on the part of Hitler, who was reluctant to sign the death warrant of his old comrade in struggle. Hitler, compassionate, had given him the choice of committing suicide. Röhm refused to do so, and a bullet in the back of the neck settled the matter. An amusing detail (if one may say so...): twenty-three years later, in 1957, his executioner, an SS policeman, was indicted by the German justice system for Röhm's murder. But he was never tried.

At the end of the "Night of the Long Knives", all opponents of Hitler within the Nazi party were ruthlessly eliminated: more than four hundred dead.

Adolf Hitler, the Führer, reigns without sharing.

He owed much of his early reign to Hjalmar Schacht.

In two ways.

First of all, on the political level: Schacht used all his influence in favor of Hitler, especially with Marshal Hindenburg. Schacht was a man who counted, both within Germany and internationally. The only German trusted by international business circles, American or English, was Hjalmar Schacht. That such a man should commit himself to Hitler is obviously a strong signal.

Hitler is also indebted to Schacht for the support he received from the financial world. The former president of the Reichsbank spared no effort to unite the big bosses of German capitalism around Hitler. Hjalmar Schacht was one of the pillars of the Keppler Circle, the Circle of Friends of the Economy (Freundeskreis der Wirtschaft), an organization of some 20 of the most powerful businessmen, a conglomerate of reactionary or right-wing bosses who solemnly asked Hindenburg to appoint Hitler as Chancellor.

Schacht also united the donors of the Nazi party around him. A fund of three million reichsmarks was set up by the Krupps, Thyssen, Schröder, Flick and Kirdorf to finance NSDAP campaigns during elections. Who was to be the administrator of this fortune? Hjalmar Schacht.

More than that, who, on a lecture tour through Europe, praised the Nazi proposals? Hjalmar Schacht. Who, during the Bad Harzburg demonstrations in which Hitler participated, expounded at length the economic program of a future Hitler government? Hjalmar Schacht.

Who finally won the decision of Marshal Hindenburg? It is more difficult to say, because the pressure came from all sides. But Hjalmar Schacht had the benefit of his successes in fighting hyperinflation, renegotiating reparations for the Great War, or scrupulously managing the Reichsbank. The voice of such a wise man in favor of Adolf Hitler certainly played a greater role in the head of state's decision than the murky maneuvers of Papen, whose reputation was already nauseating.

Schacht, Schacht, and more Schacht...

Of course, within German capitalism, Schacht was not the only one who campaigned for Hitler. Is this an extenuating circumstance for the devil's banker? Probably not. He was not the only one, but he was decisive. In the Hitler saga, his responsibility is strongly engaged, even if it is shared by others, and notably by some of the great representatives of powerful German capitalism.

Who are the other culprits, the blacksmiths, the chemical magnates, the financial moguls, who joined forces with Schacht to bring Hitler to power?

We have already mentioned Fritz Thyssen, the dinner guest at Göring's house, the Nazi who did not hate the Jews.

We could mention Emil Kirdorf, the emperor of German mines, owner of the first European mining group, who also financed Hitler. He died in 1938; Adolf Hitler, who had awarded him the highest decoration of the Nazi regime, the Order of the German Eagle, organized a state funeral for Emil Kirdorf, during which he personally laid a wreath on the grave of his wealthy protector.

Let us not forget the wealthy banker Schröder, who financed Hitler and the Nazi war effort: accused of crimes against humanity, he was sentenced to only three months in prison. During the war, he had maintained financial relations with all of Europe, enemy or friend, and in particular with the London-based Schroder's, which belonged to a branch of the family.

In the category of steelmakers, we can also dwell on the Krupp family. From the old patriarch, Gustav, to his heirs, the Krupp family provided Hitler with decisive support within German capital. Gustav's eldest son, Alfried Felix Alwyn Krupp von Bohlen und Halbach, was so committed to Hitler that he joined the SS in 1933. A solitary man and a hard worker, he compensated for his difficulties with women in business. Krupp took part in the meeting that Hitler convened with the major German capitalists a few weeks before the outbreak of war against Poland, which led to the world conflict. It was a question of distributing among the members of the German capitalist "club" the pre-annexations of companies that had been lost as a result of the Great War and the Treaty of Versailles. Krupp chose, like the others, from among the factories in those countries that had not yet been conquered. But his support for the armament effort deserved this reward: Alfried Krupp had made a specialty of transforming his factories into armament factories. Throughout the war, he remained the main supplier to the German army; the millions of dead in Hitler's campaigns in Europe and Africa owe the iron that tore their flesh to the Krupp steelworks. To manufacture their tools of death, the group's factories took advantage of an almost free labor force, deported from territories conquered by the Nazis. These workers, condemned to forced labor, were exhausted in a hundred German factories under the Krupp name. There they rubbed shoulders with about one hundred thousand slaves from the concentration camps, whose survival rate after their work experience at Krupp was close to zero. In 1948, after the war, Alfried Krupp was sentenced to twelve years in prison and the confiscation of his fortune. He was released less than three years later, in 1951, and forty-five million dollars were returned to him. Not bad... As a small consolation, women continued to make him deeply unhappy. He got married in 1952 with a beautiful vamp, Vera, but quickly separated a few months later. Perhaps Vera's appetite for the bright lights of social functions and well-built lovers had something to do with it. In the meantime, the dark and lonely Alfried Krupp had given her one of the world's largest diamonds, since then called "the Krupp". This thirty-three carat blue stone was stolen from Vera during a mugging on her ranch near Las Vegas. Found by the FBI under incredible circumstances, the diamond was bought back in 1968 by the actor Richard Burton who offered it to Elizabeth Taylor.

Another steelworker was Friedrich Flick. A man of modest origins, he had succeeded in building one of the main industrial conglomerates in Germany. A founding member of the Nazi party, he also generously financed the movement and actively participated in the conquest of power. He distinguished himself in the capture of property stolen from the Jews and in the production of armaments for the Wehrmacht and the SS: on the battlefields, whoever was not killed by a "Krupp" bullet was killed by a "Flick" bullet. Like Krupp, its factories benefited generously from the slave labor provided by the concentration camps. It is estimated that forty thousand people died of exhaustion and abuse in the Flick factories. Sentenced to seven years in prison at one of the Nuremberg trials, he was released after three years and went into business again. By 1972, when he died, Friedrich Flick was back in the top 100 fortunes of the world. The Flick family was not quite finished with its Nazi past. In 1997, Oxford University declined a donation of three hundred and fifty thousand pounds sterling because of the cursed origin of the money; a few years later, the Swiss authorities refused permission to exhibit the Flick's art collection in one of their museums. The heirs of the name were not quite finished with the law either: in 1983, the Flick son was implicated in a trial for bribing German politicians to help him evade taxes. Blood doesn't lie, and cats don't make dogs...

As for Wilhelm Keppler, he was one of the major directors of IG Farben. The Nazi regime was grateful to him for his early support of Hitler: IG Farben had the formidable privilege of manufacturing Zyklon B, the gas that was used in the gas chambers of the extermination camps. To experiment with it, the Nazis simply "delivered" five hundred Russian prisoners of war to IG Farben. The experiment having been conclusive on these unfortunate "sub-humans", because Slavs were considered as such by the Nazis, IG Farben and Heinrich Himmler's SS moved on to the industrial process in the death camps; at least three million innocent victims breathed the gas manufactured by IG Farben, initially designed to fight insects. But IG Farben made other huge profits from the war: Keppler's group annexed multiple chemical complexes in the occupied countries of Czechoslovakia, Poland, Holland, Belgium and France, where the Kuhlmann group became its property. IG Farben also benefited from the labor force in the concentration camps. In Auschwitz, two factories for IG Farben were built by the prisoners, one to produce synthetic rubber, the other to manufacture synthetic petroleum. The working conditions were appalling: woken up at three in the morning for a long walk to the construction site, the prisoners, subjected to the violence of the kapos, worked without interruption until late in the evening, without rest and fed with miserable rations. Twenty-five thousand of them lost their lives in the construction of the IG Auschwitz complex alone. Then, an agreement for the employment of the labor force represented by the people deported to the camps was duly signed between IG Farben and Heinrich Himmler's SS: the latter received three marks per day per worker, but only one and a half marks for child workers. The very idea leaves a deep unease: to think that IG Farben managers, serious men in suits and ties, who no doubt returned to their homes in the evening to kiss their wives and children, went to meetings with the SS General Staff to discuss the price of a day's work for child slaves destined to die on the job! One can imagine them: "Two marks for a child? No, that's too expensive. Our gross profit margin would be affected! What if we retained one and a half marks?

Infamous!

The living conditions, or rather the death conditions, of these workers at IG Auschwitz were hardly better than in the Auschwitz camp itself; the tens of thousands of victims were so easily replaced by the new batches of wretches of miserable people arriving each day in leaded wagons... Keppler helped Hitler to gain power, but Hitler largely paid his debt to IG Farben. Tried at Nuremberg, not at the trial of criminals against humanity, but at the so-called "ministers' trial", Wilhelm Keppler was sentenced to ten years in prison and finally released in 1951.

One could go on and on about the collusion of German capitalism with Nazism. The description of its appalling participation in war crimes and crimes against humanity is chilling. Terrifying!

As for the punishment for these crimes against humanity, it was rather light.

Of all the great capitalists who made possible the Hitler tragedy with its millions of deaths, or whose companies participated directly in these mass murders, none served more than six years in prison.

Such is the strange morality of capitalist society: the criminal who kills his neighbor is guilty. He who provides the criminal with the means to commit his crimes is not, even if he is aware that the worst horrors are about to happen.

During the war, business continued.

Chapter 6. The genius

I really like American movies.

I also like plays. In Berlin, not a week went by without my wife and I going to a play.

There is a common thread between good crime movies and successful plays: timing, pacing. The British have a very short word that perfectly describes the concept: timing, one of the favorite terms of my dear English friend Montagu Norman, the Governor of the Bank of England.

Timing is everything that makes the difference between a brilliant success and a resounding failure.

In a gangster movie, that the policeman arrives at the wrong time, and instead of killing the bandits, he kills the suspense.

In a vaudeville, if the lover comes out of the bedroom closet at the wrong moment, the funniest witticisms are no longer funny.

Timing is everything.

This is also true in economics.

A few days after his accession to the Chancellery, Adolf Hitler summoned Dr. Luther, the President of the Reichsbank, who had succeeded me in this position in 1930 after my resignation. I had known Hans Luther for twenty years. He had been Chancellor for a little more than a year, in 1925 and until May 1926. He had also been Minister of Finance, but had never succeeded in imposing himself, either with his ideas or with his authority. In this he was very much like Stresemann and Brüning: serious, normal, average, fairly honest types, but by no means cut out to be leaders, especially in times of crisis. During the Dawes negotiations, in which Hans Luther participated with me, the Allied delegates hardly noticed his presence.

Most importantly, Luther had no sense of timing.

When Luther entered the Reich Chancellor's office, which he knew well from having occupied it himself, I believe he was quite worried. The information I had from Reichsbank employees indicated the difficulties his indecision and inaccurate assessment of the economic situation created on a daily basis. In 1933, however, it was enough to drive through Berlin to immediately grasp the urgency of the situation: the country was collapsing, undermined by unemployment that affected six and a half million people. No family was left untouched by this plague. The lines at the soup kitchens had never been longer. And Luther, as a scrupulous man, president of the Reichsbank, the German central bank, was like Brüning, the former chancellor: monetary equilibrium, balanced public finances, even at the cost of a painful deflationary policy! That, according to him, was what was necessary for the country.

Adolf Hitler, I am told, asked him a single question:

- Doktor Luther, how much money can the Reichsbank mobilize immediately in order to boost economic activity and finally try to bring down this unemployment?

- Uh... Mr. Chancellor, I don't know. If I remember the situation of the Reichsbank correctly, I think we could mobilize... let's say...

between one hundred and forty and one hundred and fifty million reichsmarks?

- But that's not enough!" exploded Hitler. I would even say that it is insignificant! Doktor Luther, I can't believe that the country has reached this point! And that the Central Bank's ability to intervene has been reduced to such an extent!

- Yet, Mr. Chancellor... that is the reality. To mobilize further would weaken our situation. Not only the situation of the Reichsbank, but the situation of the entire nation. The outside world is watching us, Chancellor, because we are bound by the conditions of the Young Plan. We must respect them. I am afraid that the effort required of the Central Bank, even to the tune of one hundred and fifty million, will not be well received by the French... The Reichsbank cannot help you beyond that amount, Chancellor.

I think the discussion ended there.

Luther, like many others in his career as an economist, made several analytical errors.

In economics, there are no good and bad ideas. It's all about timing.

The best decision at one time may become the worst at another.

A deflationary policy is sometimes indispensable. When it came to stabilizing the currency in 1923, I myself pursued a deflationary policy of unprecedented violence, not hesitating to cut off all credit channels. My nickname at the time was "the gravedigger of the German economy"!

A policy of stability is sometimes the only way. In this case, it is good to have Drs. Luther in charge, for their pusillanimity, restraint and lack of initiative work wonders. They are unimaginative and risk-averse in maintaining the government budget, the value of the currency and low but steady growth.

Finally, a policy of deficits, public investment spending and economic recovery at all costs is sometimes a solution to consider, even at the cost of creating abysmal deficits.

We must be aware of the advantages and disadvantages of all the formulas; a deflationary policy will create unemployment but will boost exports and eventually reduce deficits. A policy of stability will generate speculative bubbles here and there and increase the level of latent risks. A stimulus policy will worsen the external accounts, create deficits and increase the level of debt of the state and of economic agents, but if it is well implemented, it should reduce unemployment.

All these advantages are good to take, all these disadvantages are manageable. You just have to be aware of them, know how to measure them and understand the consequences of your actions. And above all, make the right decisions at the right time!

The timing! It's all there!

In giving Hitler an answer that was full of the legendary caution of central bankers, who by tradition as well as personal inclination are madly in love with monetary stability, balanced budgets and long-term curves that slope slightly upwards, but not too much - especially not too much! - Hans Luther showed a crucial lack of sense of timing.

Indeed, what was the emergency? Certainly not the monetary situation, even if it was fragile. Certainly not the government's budgetary situation, even if it was in deficit and debts were accumulating dangerously.

The priority was unemployment, which was undermining German society.

Promising long-term stability of the state's finances to an unemployed person whose concern was to earn a few pfennig to feed his children simply did not make sense. The unemployed man needed a job! And not in the long run! Not even tomorrow! But this very evening! At dinner!

Dr. Luther could have benefited from the following lessons, all of which are lessons in timing.

First, when you have multiple challenges, you have to determine which one is the most serious and urgent, and address that one. Trying to lower unemployment without stimulus, while lowering deficits and maintaining monetary stability is a fool's errand. We might as well do nothing and let the boat drift away, begging the gods for mercy.

Secondly, for an economic policy to be effective in a crisis situation, it must mobilize all available means, even those that are not available, to tackle the causes of the crisis. There is no point in fussing! This leads to nothing! In 1923, we had to put an end to hyperinflation? Stabilization was my top priority; nothing else mattered, neither the bankruptcies I caused nor the ruins I left behind. In 1933, the problem was unemployment? The deficits, the debts, the drift of the state budget... None of this mattered! Everything had to be sacrificed to the struggle to recreate employment; never mind the financial consequences!

In the end, you will see that, in all situations, when you start to achieve results in the treatment of the problem you have targeted, the undesirable effects end up being "managed" because the adaptation capacities of the economic actors are quite strong; systematically, having solved the main problem, a kind of virtuous circle will be set up to solve the others.

Third, the economic policy you decide on must have a visible horizon. The maximum duration is five years: the results of your action must be obtained at the end of five years, not more, and preferably at the end of two or three. There is no point in having economic plans for twenty or thirty years in any field. Implementing a twenty-year reduction in unemployment? Paying off the state debt over a thirty-year horizon? This is science fiction: the only certainty you have is that in such an interval of time, many events will occur that will call into question your beautiful project: you will lose power, a new crisis will arrive, geopolitical upheavals will occur, technological innovations will change the economic landscape, etc.

Determine what the priority is; devote all possible and impossible means to solving it; have a strategy for less than five years. These are the three parameters of an economic equation that has some chance of success. And we can see that these three parameters are all questions of timing. CQFD!

Dr. Luther did not understand any of this. Hence his lack of success as Minister of Finance, Chancellor, or President of the Reichsbank.

A few days later, Adolf Hitler summoned me.

- Herr Doktor Schacht. You have experience as President of the Reichsbank. How much do you think I can expect from this institution in order to finance my investment recovery projects?

- Mr. Chancellor, I don't know!" I replied.

- You don't know? But I think the Reichsbank can provide you with figures...

- Even if I had the figures from the Reichsbank and all the major financial institutions in the country, my answer would still be the same: I don't know.

- I don't understand. Explain yourself, Doktor Schacht.

- Mr. Chancellor, I say that I do not know how many reichsmarks can be mobilized, for in view of the seriousness of the country's situation and the number of unemployed, all conceivable means must be devoted to combating this scourge. I believe that unemployment

must be defeated at all costs, and therefore the Reichsbank must provide the state with all the resources necessary to get the last of the unemployed off the streets!

My answer left him stunned. For once, Hitler remained silent. This man, for whom logorrhea was second nature, to the point that it was almost impossible to talk to him, could not find his words. And then finally:

- Herr Doktor Schacht, would you be willing to take over the presidency of the Reichsbank?

Six weeks had passed since Hitler came to power when, on March 17, 1933, I took possession of the large, bright office of the Reichsbank President.

Nevertheless, I was concerned about Hans Luther. He was one of those average, normal men who are asked to sublimate themselves in order to solve problems that are beyond them. It was not his fault that he did not have the necessary qualities; he simply should never have been there at that moment in history: a matter of timing, once again. He could not be blamed for that. He was appointed German ambassador to Paris.

Ten days after my return to the Reichsbank, I decided to make two loans to the state: one billion for the Reinhardt plan to renovate factories and housing, and six hundred million for the plan to build the Autobahnen, *that marvellous network of freeways that was to be a decisive asset, in the years that followed and up to the end of the twentieth century, in making Germany the leading economic power in Europe. This was a far cry from the hundred and fifty million reichsmarks of that brave Luther!*

A few months later, my project for the reduction of unemployment gave its first results. The country was doing a little better. Hitler, who had been so worried, began to be reassured. To speed things up, he appointed me Minister of Economics in July 1934, while keeping me as President of the Reichsbank.

With my first successes under my belt, I now had all the levers of the economy in my hand.

Because this was just the beginning!

In 1931, in the midst of the Brüning years, marked by a severe deflationary policy that resulted in six and a half to seven million unemployed, voices began to be heard calling for a change of policy direction. Brüning remained deaf to these calls, preoccupied as he was with reducing the state's deficits and the burden of debt. Moreover, he considered his freedom of movement too constrained by the very restrictive conditions imposed from outside Germany by the Allies, who relied on the Young Plan; Brüning's natural inclination was to constantly seek compromises that allowed him to avoid the radical decisions that the economic situation called for.

But within the state apparatus, there were those who called for change. Wilhelm Lautenbach was one of them.

A senior official at the Ministry of the Economy, he advocated a recovery through productive credit. Five years before the Englishman John Maynard Keynes published his *General Theory*, which would make him famous, Wilhelm Lautenbach developed what would become the core of Keynes's theories in a document entitled "The possibilities of reviving economic activity by means of investment and credit expansion".

Lautenbach was a senior civil servant. He was therefore bound by a duty of reserve and, according to the ethical rules applicable to his position, he had to approve Brüning's policy publicly or, at any rate, refrain from challenging it.

In his work, Wilhelm Lautenbach systematically countered this.

First of all, he insisted on the continual disintegration of the economy caused by Brüning's deflationary policy and on the social catastrophe that the trajectory imposed on Germany would not fail to provoke. On this point, the rest of history would obviously prove him right.

Secondly, Wilhelm Lautenbach advocated a strong increase in public debt in the short term, in order to use this credit for productive tasks, for investment, for infrastructure, and thus to re-establish the functioning of the economy, which would later generate the budgetary revenues necessary to balance the public finances again. In short, the opposite of a deflationary policy.

The Keynesian theories of stimulus through investment and increased government spending are now well known. They are studied in the first year of economics at universities all over the world, from the smallest provincial university in Uzbekistan or Burundi to Oxford and Harvard. At the time, they were a breakthrough, and Wilhelm Lautenbach was the precursor of this breakthrough. As a senior civil servant, he should have been disciplined and punished for daring to challenge the deflationary dogma of which Brüning was the apostle. But two years after his book, history was to prove him right.

The spirit of Keynes is invoked, even today, by all the true and false gurus of economics, either to insult him or to publicly adore him. A question of fashion, no doubt. As for Wilhelm Lautenbach, he never became famous. It is true that he was less interested in publicity than in serving his country, unlike Keynes, who could not live without the limelight. Lautenbach died in 1948 in Davos, Switzerland, the village that is now the annual Mecca for business stars and *chairmen of the board of* the world's major companies; fate sometimes plays with curious ironies.

When Hjalmar Schacht read Lautenbach's book, he realized that his ideas for a break in Germany's economic path were shared by others, especially in the Ministry of Economics. When the time came, he would have allies in the place to implement a productive recovery plan. But he, Schacht, was a genius. He would implement Keynes's ideas, Lautenbach's ideas, but "Schacht-style": with genius.

Once appointed to the Reichsbank and the Ministry of Economics, Hjalmar Schacht did what he knew so well: nothing.

He smokes.

He smokes a cigar.

All day.

He analyzes and reflects.

The terms of the "Schachtian" equation are as follows: how can one launch a gigantic investment plan to create six to seven million jobs in industry, construction and services, when one does not have a penny to spare? Unlike Keynes in the United Kingdom and Roosevelt in the United States, who were also launching stimulus packages at the same time and had some liquidity at their disposal, Schacht, when he arrived at the Reichsbank and the Ministry of Economics, found desperately empty coffers. It is true that at the Reichsbank he had turned the printing press on its head and granted a loan of one billion six hundred million reichsmarks to finance the initial needs of Reinhardt and Todt; but he knew that this was not enough. But the Reichsbank could not open credit lines indefinitely, unless it recreated galloping inflation, comparable to that which he, Schacht, had had to fight in 1923, and which would annihilate all efforts. Reinhardt, for industrial renovation, and Todt for highways, will soon come forward to obtain further funds; moreover, even more will have to be found for the many investment projects whose files are arriving with great regularity on the desk of the Reichsbank president.

Doing like Luther and refusing credits? Not possible.

Doing credit at all costs at the risk of recreating hyperinflation? Not possible either.

However, a solution had to be found. Roosevelt launched his *New Deal* in the United States with his dollars, Schacht will launch his *Neue Plan* in Germany without a reichsmark in his pocket! Nothing will stop him!

Hjalmar Schacht had an illumination: pre-financing. All of Germany's productive investments would be pre-financed by a mechanism outside the traditional credit of the Reichsbank. By proceeding in this way, Schacht would preserve the currency, the Reichsmark, with a certain "purity" that would guarantee it against the monetary drift that uncontrolled indebtedness would inevitably provoke. To achieve this pre-financing, the needs of which amounted to several billion per year, Schacht created an exceptionally ingenious mechanism: MEFO bonds.

MEFO stands for Metallurgische Forschungsgesellschaft. MEFO is a very small company with a very modest capital of one million Reichsmarks, founded by four giants of German industry: Krupp, which is omnipresent in Nazi history, Siemens, Rheinmetall and Gutehoffnungshütte. The pre-financing mechanism ensured that investments in industry were not financed by the state or the Reichsbank, but by the MEFO.

But, it will be objected, MEFO, with its derisory capital of one million reichsmarks, has no treasury; yet, billions of reichsmarks are needed.

Hjalmar Schacht had the answer: the investments would not be paid for in hard cash, i.e. in Reichsmarks, but in securities, the so-called MEFO bonds, which would be remunerated at a rate of 4 per cent and would be unconditionally guaranteed: one guarantee by the state, which undertook to repay the MEFO bonds on their maturity, and a second guarantee by the Reichsbank, which undertook to recount them. MEFO notes will be able to circulate in the same way as conventional money: since their redemption is guaranteed by the state and the Reichsbank, their value will be identical to that of the money in circulation.

MEFO voucher holders will understand this: they will circulate MEFO vouchers, they will exchange them, they will behave with MEFO vouchers as with reichsmarks.

The operation is a success.

In reality, Schacht created a "second" money supply dedicated solely to economic recovery. The personal aura of Hjalmar Schacht is such that even in this time of crisis, the system inspires confidence. In economics, trust is the key to success. Without Schacht, holders would have rushed to the Reichsbank to redeem the MEFO bonds, which would probably have been no better received than the requisition bonds in Belgium during the First World War, or the parallel currencies during the hyperinflation: indeed, the Metallurgische Forschungsgesellschaft would have been unable to redeem the MEFO liabilities, which would have amounted to more than a dozen billion at their peak. But with the state guarantee, added to that of the Reichsbank, and that magician Schacht to oversee it all, the MEFO bonds had a value as stable as gold.

Hjalmar Schacht's gamble paid off: he was convinced that by establishing lasting confidence in MEFO bonds, companies, industrialists, banks and even foreign investors would prefer to keep these securities in their portfolios, because they earned interest, rather than present them for redemption or discount. The banknotes hidden under mattresses, the gold coins in safes, all this money that was no longer in circulation will, over the years, be transformed into MEFO bonds and contribute to the recovery effort.

Superbly done!

The MEFO mechanism will not be the only expedient imagined by Schacht to finance productive credits, but it will be the main vector. It would allow the pump to be primed, to create the virtuous circle of confidence that gives momentum to an economic policy. Between 1934 and 1938, twelve billion reichsmarks in MEFO bonds were issued. The project that Schacht had imagined came to fruition as if by miracle, and without any pernicious drifts: no inflation, the currency was stable, unemployment was reduced...

In 1938, the seven million unemployed were no longer unemployed: as Schacht had promised Hitler, he had plucked the last of the unemployed from the streets. There was no more unemployment in Germany.

Confidence was so high that large foreign companies, which had fled Germany during the Brüning era, flocked to the party. Growth was returning to the Third Reich? Capitalists from all over the world, and especially from America, wanted to have their share.

The Rockefeller family, through the Chase National Bank and Standard Oil of New Jersey, invested in synthetic oil production and in armaments. The Nazis also received investments from Ford and General Motors.

ITT, the telecommunications and electricity company, became involved in German armaments, in particular with the manufacturer of Focke-Wulf warplanes, whose aircraft destroyed half of London during the Blitz in 1940. ITT was the same company that thirty years later was involved in the coup d'état in Chile, helping General Pinochet to overthrow and assassinate the democratically elected President Salvador Allende: big business likes dictatorships.

For the armor of their tanks and for the hulls of their warships, the Nazis massively used the Swedish steel of the industrial conglomerate Bofors, the company owned, in its time, by Alfred Nobel, which set up several production sites in Germany.

More than half of the ball bearings for the German army's war machines, turrets, engines and cannons will come from Swedish SKF Group factories in Germany.

To the rich financier Prescott Bush, founder of a famous dynasty: he is the father of the future president of the American Republic George Bush and the grandfather of the latter's son, who also became president, George Walker Bush: the man who plunged the Middle East into chaos by crushing Iraq and who justified his misdeeds with lies as outrageous as those of Hitler when he attacked Poland. Grandfather Prescott Bush, through his bank, the Union Bank, invested in several *joint ventures* with Nazi companies, notably those of Fritz Thyssen's group, among which were a number of arms factories. The Bush family thus participated in the Nazi war effort; the cannons financed by Prescott Bush contributed to bombing the GI's during their reconquest of Europe.

In short, the armament effort of the German army would probably never have been realized so quickly without the support of big international capitalism.

Schacht's determination to get the economy moving again was a brilliant success.

The first remarkable feat was to have imagined this system of pre-financing which allowed Schacht to spend money he did not have, and to have devoted it solely to productive recovery.

Schacht attracted a great deal of enmity by criticizing or even prohibiting the projects of local Nazi officials who wanted to build swimming pools, stadiums, or other investments that did not directly create jobs.

The other feat was to have succeeded in this recovery without causing the unpleasantness usually seen in a situation of economic recovery: drifting external accounts, inflation, monetary instability. Schacht achieved this by putting in place multiple regulatory constraints, controlled by a dedicated and intractable administration. He drastically restricted all imports of products not essential to industry. At the same time, raw materials, especially those useful to the arms industry, were given priority. In addition, the Reichsbank rationed all requests for foreign currency without fail; no free rides were allowed. A senior Nazi official wanted to go to London, supposedly to negotiate a trade agreement with the British, and demanded pounds sterling for this purpose? Schacht had his secretary, the devoted *Frau* Steffeck, tell him that settling the matter from Berlin with a telegram would cost no more than five reichsmarks; good German reichsmarks, at that. No foreign currency for useless and expensive travel! That day, Hjalmar Schacht, with his rigidity and condescension, made another friend...

But who cares? The rules are the same for everyone, Schacht says. Every exception to the rules means one unemployed person who remains unemployed longer. So discipline was needed, even within the Nazi party, which Schacht wanted to impress with his exemplary behaviour.

Exemplarity? When the new president arrived at the Reichsbank, he immediately renegotiated his salary. Dr. Luther had an annual stipend of two hundred thousand reichsmarks. Schacht submitted his own remuneration to a college of three ministers, who proposed that this sum be renewed.

- No! No way! Schacht throws them a mocking smile.

- Well," concedes one of them. Maybe we can do better. After all, your reputation is far superior to Dr. Luther's. How about a 30% increase?

- I refuse!

- So 40%? We can't offer you more...

- Unacceptable! Schacht hammers.

- So tell us a number, *Herr* Schacht," said another. We'll see if it's possible to go that far.

- Sixty thousand!" replies Schacht.

- Sorry?

- My remuneration will be sixty thousand reichsmarks per year! I think that's acceptable?

- But... your predecessor received two hundred thousand...

- Sixty thousand! This is my last word!

- ...

Schacht's proposal was obviously accepted. That day, the three Nazi ministers took a real lesson in exemplarity.

Hitler was euphoric. He was infinitely grateful to his great financier for having drawn the line that finally allowed the Reich to emerge from fifteen years of economic difficulties. Thanks to Schacht, prosperity returned to Germany; the people were at work and no longer thought of challenging the Nazi regime, despite its dictatorial aspects. Hitler's power owes it to Schacht that it is now installed for a long time.

But the Führer had other ambitions.

Germany must be rearmed.

The Reichswehr, the German army, must regain its former power.

In 1935, in addition to his duties as President of the Reichsbank and Minister of the Economy, Hjalmar Schacht was appointed High Plenipotentiary for Rearmament. Schacht's plan to revive the economy took on a more warlike tone: from then on, priority was given to arms and munitions factories, scientific research was directed towards the creation of new weapons, and the main objective of foreign purchases of raw materials was to rebuild the German army's logistics. Hjalmar Schacht put his own determination into this undertaking, even if he felt a certain discomfort. As a minister, he attended the councils chaired by the Führer. War was discussed. And for an economist, war means destruction, disorder, upheaval...

No discussion! The Führer ordered it! So Schacht renovated the arms factories, financed research for the bomb-carrying rockets, the *Vergeltungswaffen*, in other words the V1s that were to be launched on London, and laid the foundations for a vehicle production industry oriented towards military needs, which would become the future German automobile industry, with its flattering and very justified reputation for good quality.

Despite his effective participation in the rearmament effort, Hjalmar Schacht was not particularly popular with the Nazis, probably because he never wanted to join the party. Moreover, with Hitler's support, he did not hesitate to fall out with the main Nazi leaders.

With Heinrich Himmler, first of all: this chicken farmer managed to get into Hitler's good graces to the point of becoming the supreme chief of the SS and the Gestapo. Schacht found him vulgar and uncultured: an upstart, devoid of any scruples! For his part, Himmler, despite his sordid greed, had nothing but contempt for the financial contingencies and economic science of Schacht, who was not even a member of the Nazi party. The SS leader maneuvered unsuccessfully to remove the financier from Hitler's power circles. In 1934, Himmler was furious that Schacht was appointed Minister of Economics. He sent a messenger to intimidate him. Schacht, with his usual haughty and brittle tone, dismissed the emissary who had come to threaten him with a few contemptuous sentences. He even demanded the withdrawal of the SS guard that ensured the minister's security. He, Schacht, did not need brigands for his protection; he had Hitler.

He then became angry with Goebbels. The "little doctor," as Schacht derisively called him, could not stand the fact that Schacht competed with him in Hitler's mind as the leading intellectual of the country and of the Nazi movement. Like Himmler, whom he hated just as much, Goebbels had no regard for Schacht's qualities as an economist. He did not understand the monetary and financial lectures Schacht gave in the Council of Ministers. A fierce hatred developed between the two men; Hjalmar Schacht, in spite of his natural stiffness, tried to maintain form when they met. The Minister of Propaganda, on the other hand, did not even think about it.

Finally, he entered into competition with Göring, which is much more embarrassing. Hermann Göring, in fact, was the number two in the regime, more or less on a par with Rudolf Hess. But unlike Hess, whose intellectual capacities were very limited, Göring possessed the necessary aptitudes for his ambitions. It is true that the grandiloquent aspects of his personality, his taste for colourful uniforms, his indecent greed and the way he flaunted his wealth, tended to do him a disservice. But Göring is intelligent and manipulative. Moreover, he was consumed with ambition; the weight that Schacht was beginning to gain in Hitler's mind was beginning to bother him. For Göring, this had to stop!

Precisely at the beginning of 1936, Hjalmar Schacht began to worry about the repayment of the MEFO bonds, which were due to mature in three years' time, in 1939. The initial philosophy of his *Neue Plan* was to promote productive investments whose revenues would later allow the repayment of these bonds. But with Hitler's instructions to promote the arms industry in order to restore the reputation of the Wehrmacht, the situation was not satisfactory. Indeed, equipping an army is certainly a good thing, but it does not produce value. An army provides protection, intervention capacity or possibilities of conquest, but as long as it is armed, it only represents costs.

In the course of 1936, Hjalmar Schacht therefore began to lobby in the Council of Ministers for the imposition of spending limits for the Wehrmacht and the SS.

Outcry among ministers!

Hitler refused.

Göring was delighted; this was the opportunity he had been waiting for. He liked Schacht. But that was in the past. The past does not count for the unscrupulous ambitious.

When they first met, Hermann Göring and Hjalmar Schacht sympathized with each other; or rather, they socialized courteously. They never achieved a very high degree of intimacy, still calling each other "*Herr* Schacht" and "*Herr* Göring" even years after their first meeting, but it was not uncommon to see Schacht and his wife visiting Karinhall, the Nazi leader's sumptuous residence, where he received his guests disguised as a Roman emperor or a Wagnerian hero. Schacht did not mind Göring's ridiculous foibles; his unscrupulous greed, expressed with a certain laughing bonhomie, tended to amuse him. Göring was corruptible, that was a fact, but the fat man was intelligent, one of the few of his kind among Nazi high officials. Schacht thought he could make an ally out of him on occasion, in his discussions with Hitler.

In 1936, the relationship between the two men gradually deteriorated as Göring claimed to be involved in the economic policy of the Reich. At the National Socialist Party Congress, Hitler decreed a new economic objective: Germany must achieve autarky within four years, and Göring was in charge of this new *Vierjahresplan* ("Four-Year Plan"), which succeeded Schacht's *Neue Plan*. The reason was clear: the objective of the *Vierjahresplan* was to put the Reich in a position to wage a victorious war in Europe. Schacht was no longer the right man for the job.

For the great financier, to whom Hitler owed the consolidation of his power, the pill was hard to swallow. Göring was no longer a potential ally, but a competitor, even an enemy. Göring was all the more dangerous because, unlike Schacht, he was one of the leaders of the Nazi party, within which he enjoyed great popularity; moreover, his personal relations with Hitler made him almost unassailable.

Göring, who had just been appointed High Plenipotentiary for Planning, hastened to set up a huge administration of several hundred people in charge of implementing the *Vierjahresplan*. Of course, the relationship between this new administration and the Ministry of Economics, whose areas of responsibility were more or less the same, was not easy. The control of currency, which Schacht had made a priority, became non-existent, because the Nazi dignitaries now relied on Göring to promote their mediocre dealings. Göring was also in charge of awarding arms orders: all the big business leaders, the Krupps, the Flicks and the Thyssen, were now united around Göring: they had to make a living and keep their factories running... In fact, Schacht, who was well versed in the ruthless world of business and personally not very affectionate, understood the situation well and hardly held it against them. A form of resignation begins to win him over.

But the measure was completed the day Göring created the Hermann-Göring-Werke to personally capture part of the German mining production, which he began to have generously subsidized by the state.

No, enough is enough! It is no longer possible to conduct an economic policy worthy of the name. Göring exaggerates! Something must be done!

For his part, in order to consolidate his position in the Nazi apparatus, Göring came to the conclusion that he must definitively dismiss Hjalmar Schacht. Schacht had done a magnificent job of putting the German economy back on its feet; by taking over this work, Göring would become Hitler's undisputed second in command of the Great Reich.

The two men, who had become enemies, wanted to settle their quarrel in one way or another.

Schacht asked Hitler's secretary, Martin Bormann, for a meeting with the Führer. Bormann, with his usual bad grace and vulgarity, first dragged out the request, then, faced with Schacht's insistence on resigning, he passed it on.

It is the summer of 1937, the month of August. Hitler was vacationing in his "eagle's nest" at the Berghof, on the Obersaltzberg, that beautiful mountain near Berchtesgaden. Bormann and Göring, who also had residences nearby, often came as neighbors. On this day, several Nazi party dignitaries surrounded Hitler, who was sunbathing on the terrace. Albert Speer, the great architect, Hitler's new favorite, is there smoking a cigarette. Schacht did not like Speer very much, although he recognized his genius and rare organizational skills. A few years later, it was Speer who would administer the war economy when Schacht was no longer a renegade of the Third Reich.

Hitler led Hjalmar Schacht into his office, whose windows were wide open and overlooked the terrace where the guests were present. They all saw that Schacht, in his dark suit, hard-collared shirt and steel glasses, looked even more tense than usual. They listen carefully.

- Mr. Chancellor," Schacht began, "economic policy cannot be conducted by two such different personalities as *Herr* Göring and myself. You must decide whether you want to implement his ideas or mine. But you should know that I will not be offended in the least if you decide in favor of Göring.

- My dear Schacht," objects Hitler, "I am so grateful for what you have done. Without you, we would never have succeeded! You must come to an agreement with Göring. Make a common plan of action!

- Mr. Chancellor, *Herr* Göring's views and mine appear irreconcilable. In Germany's situation, a plan can only work with strict control of supplies and currency. Moreover, in order to satisfy the demands of the Wehrmacht, a control of the use of resources tended towards the sole production is indispensable. *Herr* Göring was not in this frame of mind.

- You are right, *Herr* Schacht, but how can you think of going away and leaving me? Think of all we have achieved together!

- Mr. Chancellor, ties are one thing, the economic inflection you wish to give the country is another," Schacht hammered, not allowing himself to be moved. If Göring's ideas are to lead this policy, my contribution is no longer necessary. But I repeat: I will not take offense. I therefore ask you to accept my resignation.

- But still, Schacht, I love you!

Adolf Hitler could not bring himself to lose such a valuable collaborator, both for his brilliant economic ideas and for his influence in international business circles. Schacht, like the guests listening on the terrace, was surprised by the Führer's curious declaration of affection. A little unsettled by Hitler's unexpected blackmail of his feelings, Schacht allows himself to be temporarily influenced: he agrees to a final negotiation with Göring.

In the two months that followed, Schacht tried to find a modus vivendi with Göring. But the fat Göring knew that he had won: that Schacht, the arrogant Schacht, the master of the economy, the man who had succeeded in everything, should put his handkerchief over his pride to negotiate with him, Hermann Göring, was a demonstration of Hitler's definitive tilt in his favor. Göring remained inflexible: it was he and no one else who would lead the *Vierjahresplan* and direct the war economy.

Hjalmar Schacht understood that he had lost the game: on November 26, 1937, his resignation from the Ministry of Economics was accepted by Hitler. He nevertheless remained president of the Reichsbank, a position from which he was relieved by Hitler a little over a year later, on January 20, 1939.

Hitler could not quite bring himself to lose Schacht; he appointed him Minister of State without portfolio, without precise responsibilities. One never knows. Hitler was lucid; Schacht had already been the providential man of the German economy three times, and it was a good idea to keep him in reserve if a fourth rescue was necessary one day. Especially since the Führer was perfectly aware that with Walther Funk, Göring's protégé, whom Göring wanted to make his chief man in charge of the economy, he was no longer in the same category as Schacht.

Ah, that Göring!" sighed Hitler. If only he could have got along with Schacht!

The day Göring took over the Ministry of Economics, he could not resist the urge to make one last boast at Schacht's expense. He had him call the Reichsbank on the telephone:

"Herr Schacht? I am now sitting on your chair!" he laughs.

Hjalmar Schacht did not answer and hung up.

There is no room in Schacht's modus operandi for antics. The great financier sighs and gets back to work.

The two men would not see each other again until the end of Hitler's adventure.

Their reunion took place in Nuremberg, during their trial for crimes against humanity. In the prison where they were held, the prisoners were entitled to one bath per week.

On this day, a GI leads the old Schacht to the bathroom cell where two bathtubs are installed.

Schacht undresses and begins to wash himself.

The door opens; enters a guard with another prisoner.

Hermann Göring.

Her soap in hand.

Chapter 7. The accomplice

I, Hjalmar Schacht, have always remained a stranger to the persecution of these poor Jews during the Hitler years. On the contrary, I despise the thoughtless hatred directed at these people.

Sometimes I indulged in gourmet pleasures at the expense of those compulsive anti-Semites who, in cohorts as dense as the clouds of mosquitoes in the swamps at the mouth of the Elbe, swirled in tight clouds around Adolf Hitler. One of my favorite stooges was Gottfried Feder, the "economist" who gave himself that title without having the slightest idea of how the economy worked, but who had nevertheless managed to become Hitler's financial advisor. Feder was the inspiration for the indigestible paragraphs of anti-Semitic gobbledygook in Mein Kampf, which serve as an economic program for the recovery of the German nation.

When I had made six hundred million Reichsmarks available to finance the construction of highways in 1933, Hitler asked my advice:

- I have two candidates to lead the Reichsautobahnen (RAB), which will build the highway network: Todt and Feder. What do you think of them?

- Unquestionably, Mr. Chancellor, I recommend Todt to you," I said forcefully.

- How?" said Hitler, astonished. Do you know Todt?

- No, not at all. But I know Feder!

This is how Fritz Todt became the grand master of German roads and, later, the head of the Todt Organization, which directed the Wehrmacht's armament program from 1940 onwards, which I myself had financed.

But my little arrow had not quite killed Feder, whom I met again when I was appointed Minister in 1934, as Secretary of State at the Ministry of Economics. He was to become my deputy, but his convictions had not changed much: every note from the departments supervised by the eminent Gottfried Feder transpired his visceral anti-Semitism. Without missing a beat, on the day of my appointment, I summoned him to my office:

- Herr *Feder*, please note that as of today, your duties at the Ministry of Economics are terminated.

- But, Mr. Minister," Feder protested, "I can assure you that I am ready to collaborate with you with the utmost loyalty!

- That may well be, Herr *Feder*. But not me!

Gone was Feder the anti-Semite. This time I had got him; he was removed from the circles of Nazi power and left to make himself forgotten as a professor at a provincial university. I felt sorry for his unfortunate students from a distance; may they have given him a hard time, as the gossips know so well how to do.

I should not be held responsible for these little misdeeds. They were aimed at much more wicked people.

The Stürmer, *the newspaper headed by Julius Streicher, regularly launched its most vile anti-Semitic attacks against me or my collaborators. More than once I had to intervene, if necessary by appealing to Hitler himself, to stop the infamy that the* Stürmer *was spreading against such and such a member of the Reichsbank or another member of the Ministry of Economics, accused of being Jewish or of doing business with Jewish companies. I found Streicher many years later in Nuremberg, in the dock of the court of crimes against humanity. Despite the passage of time, despite the horrors of the war that had marked us all, he had not changed one iota.*

Scary Julius Streicher! Every edition of the Stürmer *carried the motto* Die Juden sind unser Unglück *(The Jews are our misfortune) at the bottom of the first page in large letters. His rag was nothing but vulgarity and pornography. To think that it was read by half a million of my fellow citizens! I believe that Streicher was above all a pathological case; his hatred of the Jews was more akin to psychiatry. He was probably irresponsible and his vicious personality expressed all his perversity in his hatred of Jews. Streicher should have been treated; instead, he was hanged. I was told that his execution was particularly abominable, not unlike the fate he advocated for the unfortunate Jews.*

As for the little Dr. Goebbels, his fiery speeches against international Jewry were masterpieces of obscurantism and irrationality. In 1933, he had twenty thousand books called "Jewish" burned in front of the Berlin Opera House. At Nuremberg in 1935, before the Nazi legions parading with torches and flags, he proclaimed that a Jewish conspiracy existed internationally to destroy Western civilization. Such a bold profession of faith should have been laughed at. Instead, it was acclaimed. Goebbels was the inspiration for the violent demonstrations against the Jewish community, for no other reason than his relentless desire to do away with those people he did not like. And to think that the little doctor claimed to be the first intellectual in the country! He hated me because I was in his shadow.

But he had a certain intelligence of the absurd in his detestation of the Jews. Thus, in order to exclude them from the artistic professions that came under his ministry, Goebbels did not use the direct method that would have consisted in forbidding them from these activities. The little doctor, Minister of Propaganda, demanded that all actors, writers, musicians and journalists join the Reichskulturkammer, *the Reich Chamber of Culture. At the same time, he forbade non-Aryan individuals to join the* Reichskulturkammer. *As a result, there were no Jews in Berlin's theaters, and no music by Jewish composers was played by orchestras. The artists chose to leave, starting with the great Kurt Weil, the composer of my favorite show,* Die Dreigroschenoper *("The Threepenny Opera").*

For my part, I have always considered the Nazi regime's policy towards the Jews to be a serious mistake. First of all, because it discredited the regime in the eyes of my external partners. When I toured the United States and Europe, many people asked me about the mistreatment of Jews in Germany. Many opportunities to make business connections were lost because of this violence. In addition, the destruction of stores, homes, and schools was a loss of value to the economy, which did not need it. Finally, some of these Jews had important functions for the economy. To drive them out was to deprive the productive system of a substantial work force as well as of valuable know-how. Even if the Jews no longer had a place in our society, all these economic consequences had to be considered before deciding to exclude them.

I pleaded this thesis before Hitler. I thought I was heard, but in reality I was not heard. Hitler had guaranteed me, when I was appointed Minister of Economics, that I would not have to worry about the Jewish problem. Experience showed that the problem was not so much economic as philosophical, and as a senior official I could not escape it.

I looked for solutions; my plan for the emigration of the Jews from German territory could have saved many lives; this is realized today, but I am not given much credit.

Hjalmar Schacht did not like Jews.

He doesn't have anything particular to blame them for, but he doesn't like them. That's just the way it is. There's nothing rational about it.

The Jews were different, they were poorly integrated into German society, they cultivated their religious specificity, they had social habits that set them apart.

So they're a bit of a nuisance.

We don't like them.

So Schacht doesn't like them.

Oh, well, if one were to take the time to examine them objectively, one would realize that in reality they were not much trouble. And especially not Hjalmar Schacht; besides, Schacht cultivated many connections among the Jews. How could it be otherwise in finance? Jews are everywhere. His boss at the Danat Bank was a Jew, Jakob Goldschmitt. Several of its directors at the Reichsbank are Jews. Many of the officials at the Ministry of Economics were Jews. Schacht worked well with them. He appreciated their accuracy at work, their good understanding of financial affairs, their loyalty to his instructions. They were excellent collaborators! Schacht could only congratulate himself on their services. Moreover, when his personal or professional acquaintances among the Jews were attacked, Schacht always defended them, not hesitating to go to the highest levels of government to put an end to the harassment imposed on them.

But it doesn't matter! As soon as he is asked about Jews in general, Schacht cannot hide the fact that he does not like them.

We must remember the context of the time.

Rightly, anti-Semitism, that idiotic manifestation of hostility towards a person or a people because of their religion, is now a crime. In the 1930s, it was almost a norm, and not only in Germany. In France, the Dreyfus affair had set one part of the country against the other; it was nothing but a manifestation of anti-Semitism. In Poland, anti-Semitism was endemic. Jews traditionally lived separately from the rest of the population, in villages that only they inhabited or in parts of the cities, the ghettos, that were reserved for them. In Russia, the same was true, and pogroms, i.e., hunts for Jews, often with many victims, took place from time to time. In all the great cities of Europe, Prague, Bucharest, Venice, Rome, districts were reserved for the Jews, who were thus subjected to a kind of ordinary ostracism.

In the press, "international Jewry," that odious and stupid term, was a concept taken up in many publications, *Action Française* in Paris, *Avanti!* in Rome, and of course in the Nazi newspapers in Germany.

In short, anti-Semitism was a widely shared, even tolerated, state of mind, which was most often expressed more or less neutrally, simply by imposing a certain social separation, but sometimes also with animosity, even extreme violence, as in Germany, but also in Poland or Russia.

In this respect, Hjalmar Schacht was in tune with the times. In his writings, when he evokes such and such a person of the Jewish faith, they are almost systematically described as "Jews", as if this personality trait had a particular importance. One would look in vain in his books for the same reference to Catholics, Protestants,

Orthodox, Unionists, Baptists, Anglicans, Muslims, etc. However, in the course of his travels, Hjalmar Schacht encountered representatives of all religions and ethnic groups; but only the "Jews" are ostracized in this way, and Schacht systematically points out the alleged defects of this population.

Schacht frequently insisted on the problem they represented. Hence, often, his ambivalence towards the Jewish question and the ambiguity of his conduct towards them. For Hjalmar Schacht, there was indeed a "Jewish problem"; and this problem had to be solved.

But in a reasonable way.

Others had much less restraint.

Especially those who met in Wannsee one day in January 1942, while Schacht, sixty kilometers away, in his estate in Gühlen, was moping in boredom, because at that time Hitler kept him away from the centers of power.

The district of Wannsee, in the southeast of Berlin, is probably the most beautiful suburb of the German capital. A network of lakes, islands and forests form a small paradise just a few minutes away from the hectic life of the big city. Luxury, calm and pleasure reign here; when summer comes, Berliners love to go to Wannsee to enjoy the long June evenings under the foliage of birch trees and weeping willows. Families picnic and lovers kiss on the lakeside lawns.

In winter, Wannsee falls asleep under the snow and waits for spring.

On January 20, 1942, Reinhard Heydrich, the deputy of Heinrich Himmler, head of the SS, organized a conference in Wannsee, in the Villa Marlier, with fourteen other dignitaries of the Third Reich.

The same day, much further east, Soviet Marshal Zhukov led a victorious offensive around Moscow. He routed the Wehrmacht, which retreated two hundred kilometers. It has been seven months since Hitler launched Operation Barbarossa against the Soviet Union, and three months since the Battle of Moscow. Until now, the Axis forces have pushed the Communist armies aside, conquering Ukraine and Belarus one after the other and arriving at the gates of Moscow. This day of January 1942 is the turning point of the war: pursued by the Siberian battalions, weakened by this intense cold for which they were not prepared, the German forces begin a retreat that will stop only three years later, in the ruins of Berlin, a few kilometers from the Marlier villa. The battle of Moscow, which ended on that January day, remains the largest battle in the history of mankind, far ahead of Stalingrad: six hundred and fifteen thousand German soldiers and nine hundred and fifty-eight thousand Russian soldiers lost their lives.

January 20, 1942, was therefore an essential day in the course of the war.

This same day is also an essential date of the Jewish genocide.

However, if you think about it, for the Jewish populations of Europe, this historic date does not change their fate, because for several years they have been subjected to a terrible martyrdom that will only end with the final defeat of the Nazi regime. But January 20, 1942, the day of Russian glory and German defeat in Moscow, remains engraved in the common memory of humanity as one of the most shameful days in its history: the day of the "Wannsee Conference.

That day, Reinhard Heydrich was far from the frenzy and the deafening noise of the bombs that rained down on the German armies around the Soviet capital in the icy air. The Villa Marlier is perfectly quiet in the cold air of Wannsee. Comfortably seated in the large living room heated by a warm fire, Heydrich ordered tea from the maitre d' for everyone present.

He then opened the floor for discussion.

There were representatives from most of the ministries: the Interior, Foreign Affairs, Economy, the Ministry for the Eastern Territories, the Party Chancellery, the Reich Chancellery, and the various Gestapo departments in charge of Jewish affairs: Adolf Eichmann, the official of the Final Solution, was there, as was Heinrich Müller, the great Gestapo chief. Two SS men represented the General Government of Poland, a country with so many Jews. The Ministry of Justice sent the sinister Dr. Roland Freisler, a half-crazy man who, a few months later, would preside over the "People's Court" (Volksgerichthof), a sort of special court of justice of the Reich, more precisely a political court charged with condemning opponents of the Nazi regime for high treason and undermining state security. The conspirators of the last of the attacks against Hitler (July 20, 1944), those of Operation Valkyrie of Colonel Count von Stauffenberg, were handed over to the hysteria of Freisler.

Why this gathering of officials and lawyers?

The Wannsee Conference was not intended to decide on the extermination of the Jews, in other words, on the "final solution of the Jewish question". The annihilation of the Jews had already been decided and had begun to be implemented. Five hundred and thirty thousand Jews had already emigrated from Germany. Two participants in the meeting, *SS-Sturmbannführer* Rudolf Lange, head of the Security Service (Sicherheitsdienst) in Latvia, and *SS-Oberführer* Schöngarth, head of the Sicherheitspolizei in Poland, had already personally taken part in the "Shoah by bullets", the massacre by pistol or machine gun of the Jewish population behind the front lines of the territories conquered by the army. A horror without a name, this "Shoah by bullets". "The mass murder of men, women and children caused psychological problems for the SS officers in charge of the executions," said Lange and Schöngarth to their colleagues. This was very unfortunate!

No, it's not about deciding.

The decisions to put an end to the Jews of Europe for good had already been taken by Hitler, Himmler and others. It was a question of organization and administration. In order to exterminate the eleven million Jews in the countries that the Third Reich had conquered, or that Hitler still intended to conquer, the general principle was to transfer them to the East. They would preferably be deported beyond Poland, that is to say to Russia, when that country was conquered and occupied. Then the idea is to put these *Untermenschen* to work. In a first step, after a first physical elimination of the weakest according to an adequate process to be defined, the able-bodied will be used to build roads, with working and living conditions that should allow a substantial reduction of their number. Then it will be necessary to eliminate the remainder with adapted methods.

A well-structured master plan, which Adolf Eichmann was charged with putting into music with the relevant logistical means.

Among these zealous officials, some debates arose about special situations: what to do with half-Jews, quarter-Jews, Jews who had converted to other religions? How should Jews married to non-Jews be treated? It is necessary to foresee the different cases, to have procedures for each situation, to consider the treatment of exceptions. The jurists in the group discuss these points of detail, exchange arguments, and then agree on compromises as to the fate of these marginal cases.

The machine for crushing men now has an administrative and regulatory framework that keeps the ministries happy.

Satisfied, the conference participants parted ways. The senior officials bundled up in their overcoats and the SS in their uniform coats. They left in the cold of Wannsee, happy with the meeting, which had been efficiently discussed and decided upon. Heydrich and Eichmann remained alone in the Marlier villa. They sighed at the magnitude of the task: all those millions of men, women and children to be wiped out, what an immense task to plan! So many corpses to burn!...

In reality, the Wannsee Conference did not really change anything. Neither the fate of the Jews, whose final extermination had already been ratified by the Führer and his abominable thurifers, nor the Nazi practice of treating the Jews. The Third Reich was only concerned with giving a legal appearance to its appalling crimes; a matter, no doubt, of tradition. In Nazi Germany, things had to be organized, documented, proceduralized, even in the darkest aspects of its crimes.

Those committed against the Jewish population are beyond imagination.

There were three main periods in the anti-Semitic intensity of Hitler's regime.

The arrival in power in 1933 marked a first phase: boycott of stores, beatings of owners, broken shop windows, houses covered with swastikas... It was the initial phase, the lifting of inhibitions, the expression of frustrations: a type of behavior that is frequently found when the extreme right comes to power, and this in all countries.

We shall return to the second phase, the one in which Schacht's name is involved.

The third phase was intended to be terminal: it opened with the "Kristallnacht" in 1938 and continued with the Shoah, the Wannsee Conference and the industrialization of the process of destruction of the Jewish population in the death camps. The triggering event was the assassination in Paris of a German embassy attaché by a young Jew. Goebbels launched the Nazi legions and all their sympathizers into the assault on the population: devastated stores, molested families, spoliations, assassinations, the first deportations... until the systematization of the extermination policy to which the Wannsee conference gave a legal envelope that satisfied the Cartesian mind of the death officials.

At the time of Wannsee, Hjalmar Schacht was only a minister without portfolio and without power, who hardly ever left his estate in Gühlen. Therefore, he was not involved in the meeting or in the extermination policy in any way.

But there is the second phase.

It began when Schacht was Minister of the Economy and President of the Reichsbank, and moreover one of Hitler's most listened-to advisors.

The one in which the powerful financier, who did not want to get his hands dirty, will participate to preserve his power.

The second phase of the Nazi regime's active anti-Semitism began with the Nuremberg Laws and the Nazi party congress held in that city in 1935, seven years before Wannsee. Hjalmar Schacht was at the height of his power, his influence on the Führer and his fame as the greatest financier of the century. In the conference room of the party headquarters building, Schacht sat at the podium and presided.

"Gentlemen! I declare the meeting open!" proclaims Hjalmar Schacht. "Today we will consider the laws that will permit the separation of the Jews from the German population of the Reich."

The cream of the Nazi gotha was gathered at Nuremberg: in the assembly presided over by Schacht, one could recognize Reinhard

Heydrich, Himmler's deputy, who represented the SS, Wilhelm Frick, Minister of the Interior, Franz Gürtner, Minister of Justice, Johannes Popitz, Prussian Minister of Finance, Adolf Wagner, Bavarian Minister of the Interior, and others.

Under the leadership of Schacht, the only non-party member among them, these Nazi high-plenipotentiaries gathered to discuss the racial laws prepared to put an end to the outbreaks of anti-Jewish violence that had taken place over the past few months: Jewish markets had been ravaged by the SA and SS, Jewish schools had been ransacked by members of the Hitler Youth, and Jews had been beaten, sometimes to death. In some cities administered by particularly virulent Nazis, Jews were banned from libraries, cinemas and public transport. In short, an atmosphere of pogroms took hold in Germany a few months before the Berlin Olympics, scheduled for the summer of 1936. Abroad, many voices were raised to protest against the mistreatment of Jews in Germany. However, Hitler was very concerned about the success of the Berlin Olympic Games, which were to consecrate the rebirth of eternal Germany, a rebirth of which he, the Führer, was the hero.

The racial laws were intended to replace uncontrolled violence with state violence: from then on, marriages between Jews and citizens of German blood were prohibited, extramarital sexual relations were a crime, Jews could no longer employ German domestic staff, and Jews were no longer German "citizens" (*Staatsbürger*) but only "nationals" (*Staatsangehörige*).

Subsequently, a series of decrees supplemented these laws and gradually prohibited Jews from practicing many professions: dentist, civil servant, cab driver, etc. Several of these decrees were signed by Hjalmar Schacht.

The latter's attitude is very equivocal. On the one hand, the politician could not refuse to obey Hitler's injunctions and the pressures of the Nazi party. But on the other hand, the financier could not agree to unbalance the economy by simply stopping whole sections of the country's activity that were carried out by the Jews. So he moderated, he delayed, he let some businesses and professions survive for a few more months before giving in.

Ambivalence, ambivalence... Schacht did not like the Jews, but he was not a rabid anti-Semite. In his speeches, he pleads for the departure of the Jews, who according to him no longer have a place in German society, but for an orderly departure. He was resolutely hostile to those who massacred Jewish families in a barbaric manner, as during *Kristallnacht*, the "Kristallnacht" unleashed by Goebbels. On the night of November 10-11, 1938, two hundred and eighty synagogues were burned down, seven thousand five hundred Jewish businesses were destroyed and thirty thousand people were arrested and deported. The Jewish community was collectively fined one billion Reichsmarks and all the businesses it still controlled had to be "Aryanized".

A disaster for business, deplored Schacht: in addition to the damage in the country, Germany's economic partners, outraged, cancelled their orders to industry, put an end to supply contracts, and withdrew their capital from German banks. An economic catastrophe, this "Kristallnacht"!

But what could he do? In 1938, Schacht had lost almost all his influence in the management of the German economy to Hermann Göring; after the "Kristallnacht", the latter issued the last decrees that definitively forbade Jews from any economic or professional activity in Germany.

This is the point of no return.

Remembering that he was an economist, Hjalmar Schacht, who was still president of the Reichsbank for a few months, made one last attempt to settle the Jewish question in an "orderly" manner. With Hitler's agreement, under the pretext of a private visit to his friend Montagu Norman, the governor of the Bank of England, he met in England with two delegates of the Jewish community, an American from New York, Samuel Rubbee, and the Englishman Lord Berstead, a wealthy businessman. Schacht proposed the emigration of all Jews from Germany to Palestine; only the elderly would be allowed to remain on German territory. The financier had planned everything: the cost of the logistical operations would be financed by means of an international loan pledged on the goods that the Jews would leave in Germany.

To tell the truth, this plan was not new. Several projects had been prepared, more or less seriously, to deport the German Jewish population, either to Rhodesia, to Madagascar, or to other exotic destinations such as British New Guinea (present-day Papua New Guinea). Reinhard Heydrich, the man from Wannsee, had himself been the promoter of a deportation project to Madagascar, which was finally abandoned when France refused. After the French defeat in June 1940, Heydrich's deputy, Adolf Eichmann, tried for a while to revive the project - the French authorities having been made more pliable by the occupying forces - but he did not persist in the project. The Final Solution was launched and nothing could stop it.

Schacht's proposal, on the other hand, had the merit of having been prepared "Schacht-style", i.e., of being perfectly realistic, financed, organized, administered. The two Jewish delegates listened to him. But could they trust this man, a loyal supporter of the Nazi regime, a signatory of the anti-Semitic Nuremberg laws and the anti-Jewish decrees, and, moreover, dispatched by Hitler?

They rejected the offer.

The ultimate snub: the pretext they found for declining the Schacht plan was financial. The British indicated that, in their opinion, the balance of resources and needs established by Schacht was unbalanced and that, in the absence of adequate financing, it was not possible to proceed. Unbalanced financing! To say that to him, Hjalmar Schacht, the greatest financier of the century! Was there no value left in this world?

But in the end, the devil's banker was only moderately surprised. Did he himself believe in this plan? His aura with Hitler was singularly wavering, his influence in the government was disappearing to the benefit of Göring and Funk, so it was understandable that he did not win over the Jews.

Schacht went to Berchtesgaden to report his failure to the Führer, who barely listened.

A few months later, when he was removed from his position as president of the Reichsbank, he went on a trip to the East to get a change of scenery, far from Germany and the anti-Jewish persecutions that were dramatically increasing. In Turkey, Iran, and India, he was received with the pomp of a sovereign, even though he was no longer anything. In these countries, he had kept the image of a great man. Schacht returned to Germany. Montagu Norman advised him to emigrate because of the risks to his safety: England or the United States would probably be happy to welcome him. But no, not a chance: reassured by the success of his trip, he preferred to stay in Germany.

He retired to Gühlen. The Jewish question was no longer an issue for him. He was probably relieved.

Ultimately, it remains difficult today to form an opinion on Hjalmar Schacht's responsibility for the Nazi regime's iniquitous treatment of the Jews and the Holocaust.

Innocent? Guilty? Aiding and abetting?

Is it that simple? Before the Nuremberg Tribunal and during the denazification trials, Schacht invariably expressed his denial of responsibility for Hitler's rise to power. Similarly, he always claimed to have been a perfect stranger to anti-Semitic politics.

He was not the only one.

At the Nuremberg trial, almost without exception, all the defendants claimed to have never been aware of the horrors of the extermination camps: even Göring, even Kaltenbrunner, Himmler's deputy who replaced Heydrich after his assassination in Prague, all claimed to have never been aware of what was happening in the camps. Only Hans Frank, the *gauleiter* of Poland, promoter of the extermination camps of Majdanek, Treblinka, Sobibor and Belzec, admitted that he was not unaware that these camps were used for the mass destruction of human beings. It should be noted, however, that these general denials came after the terrible images of these mass graves, of living skeletons, of emaciated children, of the barbaric abomination that some men had inflicted on other men, their wives and children, had been projected in the courtroom. Psychiatrists who study major criminals have often written about this: faced with the horror of the acts committed, the human mind, in a defensive reaction, refuses to admit the existence of responsibility, or even the existence of the crime, so unbearable is it.

This unbelievable generalized denial extended to the entire German population: the real culprits were Hitler and Himmler. They were dead. The rest of us didn't know anything about it. The line of defense was quite practical.

This was obviously not true.

Hjalmar Schacht, Hitler's financier, such an important official in the government apparatus, could not remain aloof from such a crucial aspect of the exercise of Nazi power. But what was his degree of personal responsibility? Schacht, by the standards of the time, was not a militant anti-Semite. He just didn't like Jews. When the Führer asked him to preside over the launching of the Nuremberg racial laws or to sign the ordinances excluding Jews from certain professions, he complied. At the same time, he defended Jewish collaborators or acquaintances and made a good-faith effort to launch his plan to save the German Jewish people. More than the exclusion itself, he deplored the economic consequences of the brutal exclusion of the Jews from society, to which he was not fundamentally opposed. In fact, on several occasions he had stated that the place of the Jews was no longer in Germany, and he reaffirmed this before the Nuremberg Tribunal.

However, he deplored the methods used.

Did he know the exact reality of the extermination? Why didn't he follow the same path as Fritz Thyssen, fleeing to Switzerland? In 1938, at the time of *Kristallnacht*, Schacht was already in semi-disgrace. He could have fled, therefore, in order not to endorse the misdeeds of the savage hordes of Goebbels and others. He did not. The fault, no doubt, lies in his high opinion of himself: Schacht could not believe that his disgrace would become total and that he would no longer be able to influence events.

But he knew.

There is no doubt that Hjalmar Schacht was aware of arbitrary imprisonments, deportations and executions. As head of the Reichsbank, he financed the programs of the Reichswehr and the SS. He financed the trains, he financed the purchase of land, materials, in short, the logistics necessary for the operation of the camps. Schacht was so meticulous about control that the slightest outflow of currency was examined by his administration. The latter inevitably passed on information to its highest official. How could Schacht, who moreover attended the council of ministers, have been unaware of the drama that was unfolding?

The same reasoning applies to the German nation. The legend of a German people who knew nothing about the camps and the Holocaust has long circulated. No doubt they were not aware of the exact reality of the tragedy that was played out in Dachau or Auschwitz. But can we imagine a population totally blinded? Because in addition to being a satanic extermination enterprise, the Holocaust organized by the Nazi government was an immense administration. It required considerable means and a very Germanic organization to achieve this unheard-of result: six million dead. Six million dead! How many Germans worked to achieve this result? How many typists typed lists of names, how many policemen read them on their way to arrest the unfortunate victims, how many railroad workers drove the trains loaded with human cattle on their way to the slaughterhouse, how many secretaries organized the transport schedule, how many station managers saw the convoys go by, how many Reichsbahn accountants drew up the invoices, how many chemists produced and delivered the Zyklon B, how many suppliers brought their goods to Treblinka or Flossenbürg, how many mayors seized the apartments of the Jews in order to reallocate them, how many letter carriers went back to their homes to keep the mail of families that would never be seen again, how many tax inspectors crossed out the missing persons from the registers of taxpayers, how many bakers were astonished that the little boy from the Goldbergs, that smiling boy, did not come to fetch the bread from one day to the next, how many, how many?... All these good people, associated in one way or another with the Jewish genocide or its consequences, had families, friends, children, relatives. Can we imagine that in private, they never shared their questions, gave their testimony, discussed their experience? And that from far and wide, the astonishment at the disappearance into the ether of hundreds of thousands of compatriots, neighbors and friends did not arouse the slightest curiosity?

Didn't anyone notice anything?

Nobody understood?

Nobody knew?

There is no one more blind than the one who does not want to see...

Of course, it was not a safe time. You had to avoid being noticed. Not far away, the Nazi *blockleiter*, that filthy bastard with his swastika, was just waiting for an opportunity to denounce you... So keep quiet!

Hjalmar Schacht, meanwhile, in the peace and quiet of Gühlen, remembered that he had presided over the Nuremberg racial laws in the midst of similar filthy bastards. He had signed the ordinances forbidding Jews to practice their profession.

Like an ordinary bastard.

Chapter 8. The conjurer

When I was relieved of my duties as Minister of Economics in favor of Göring, and Göring began to sacrifice my work of stabilizing Germany to the war effort, I realized how harmful Adolf Hitler's dictatorship was to the Reich. I decided that I, Hjalmar Schacht, would put an end to his rule. So I made the necessary contacts with a few people to prepare the conditions for a coup.

The least we can say is that I was not helped by the circumstances. Nor, for that matter, by the other participants in the plot. I was struck by the amateurishness and lack of resolve of some of the senior officials on whom I thought I could rely.

Carl Goerdeler, for example. This politician was a charming, honest man, devoted to the cause of the public good and endowed with solid personal convictions, both religious and political and economic. Some were very defensible, such as his opposition to Nazism. Others were perfectly absurd; I remember with amusement the open opposition he showed me, when I was Minister of the Economy and he was Commissioner for Prices, concerning my policy, which he considered inflationary. To come and reproach me,

Hjalmar Schacht, for pursuing an inflationary policy! Really, at that time, some people had no common sense!

But I did not hold it against him; when in 1938 I began to prepare the plot against Hitler, I contacted him. I must admit that I sometimes regretted it: this incorrigible talker endangered the operation with his carelessness. He could not help writing letters in which he spoke in hushed tones about our plans, or holding conversations, even in public, in which he spoke with his eternal optimism about the coming end of the Nazi regime. May he be forgiven: his martyrdom, tortured for months by the Gestapo, and his death by beheading, just three months before the end of the war, would have justified his being canonized.

The ones who disappointed me the most were the military. We obviously needed them to overthrow Hitler, and I was counting on General Erwin von Witzleben, that great soldier, then military governor of Berlin, to bring the capital of the Reich under control. Witzleben's straight and clear gaze was a great comfort to me: torn between my duties at the Reichsbank, my obligations as a minister, even without portfolio, and the preparations for the conspiracy, I was under a nervous tension that was truly inhuman. Sometimes, when I met Hitler or Funk, I had the feeling that they were looking at me and thinking, "I know what you are up to!" Fortunately, Witzleben's determination confirmed that our path was the right one.

He introduced me to Halder. It was a terrible disappointment. However, Franz Halder was a major general and number two in the Wehrmacht General Staff. He was strictly incapable of making a decision. We were not sure whether we could count him in or not. His only contribution was to introduce us to his superior, Walther von Brauchitsch, the commander-in-chief of the army, but he did not give us any further support:

- I will do nothing for you, gentlemen, he assured us. I will not prevent you from acting, but do not count on the help of my troops.

- We are not asking you to mobilize the Wehrmacht! The question is what you, Brauchitsch, will do when we start the operation.

- Are you going to assassinate Hitler?

- No, there is no question of that! He will be arrested and a new government with Dr. Schacht at its head will be appointed! It's about preventing war, Brauchitsch!

- Under these conditions, you know my answer: I will not oppose your action, but I will not do anything to promote it.

We could not get anything else out of it.

Brauchitsch was terrorized by Hitler. Every meeting with the Führer was an ordeal for him; for a soldier of his rank, his ability to fight was microscopic. He behaved like a rug and was surprised that the Führer trampled on him. Yet the man was intelligent: he conceived the blitzkrieg plan that brought France to its knees in the spring of 1940. But he never helped us; on the contrary, he finally betrayed us by demanding in writing that all his generals cease all criticism of Hitler. He was rewarded with a promotion to the rank of Generalfeldmarschall. But he did not denounce us, probably out of respect for Witzleben.

In the end, those who sabotaged our plot were Neville Chamberlain and Edouard Daladier. By signing the Munich Agreement in September 1938, which allowed Hitler to annex the Sudetenland region of Czechoslovakia, the British and French prime ministers made it impossible to take political action against Hitler: he had become a national hero and his popularity in Germany was at its peak. The cowardice of the French and the British had allowed him to tear Czechoslovakia apart without firing a shot. War was no longer an immediate prospect and Hitler felt he had a free hand in Europe.

He was triumphant.

We gave up.

Our action would have stopped the march to war and restored a democratic republic in Germany. But Hitler had been favored by fate. The lucky star never left this demon. During the following years, while I stayed mostly in my estate in Gühlen, I remained in contact with the resistance against Hitler and was informed about some of the plots. But none of the attempts to end his rule were successful. In each case, the military, who had disappointed me so much during the project I had organized in 1938, failed in the plans they had made without me.

I was convinced that the military are not cut out for conspiracies. They know how to obey, they know how to transmit orders, but to take initiatives that go beyond their pre-established mental patterns inscribed in their genes since their classes as officer cadets is another story. A general knows how to build a battle plan: deployment of forces, setting up of logistics, execution of the plan and, depending on success or failure, subsequent option: continuation of the advance or tactical withdrawal to pre-prepared positions. But few generals know how to practice like an economist; I mean, a good economist, not a half-wit like those who unfortunately populate governments. To succeed, there is only one method: to make a drastic choice based on the sole conviction that the planned scheme will work, and to devote all one's resources to it with no possibility of turning back. In the economic field, when I defeated hyperinflation by ruining part of the financial sector, when I revived the German economy and put an end to unemployment by creating billions of MEFO bonds, there was no turning back. Going forward was the only alternative.

It is said that Hernán Cortès, when he landed in South America with his conquistadors, had his ships burned in order to forbid any return.

A military man cannot think like that. He must plan escape routes, emergency exits, fallback positions. His mental scheme requires him to envisage failure and to calculate the consequences of this failure; by practicing this way, he also multiplies his chances of failure.

Hitler survived sixteen attacks. Another great leader was equally lucky: French General Charles de Gaulle. I was an old man when he came to power in France in 1958. After he granted independence to Algeria, the military formed a secret organization and made several attempts to assassinate him. But they failed in each attempt, because their strategy was typically military: by over-planning the evacuation of troops and escape routes, the retreat ended up being more important in the plot than the objective itself. As a result, the chances of not achieving it multiplied.

Burn out his vessels.

Brauchitsch refused to do so and was forgotten.

Cortes, on the other hand, went down in history.

Hitler's strategy was announced in *Mein Kampf*, the book in which Adolf Hitler delivered his *Weltanschauung*, his "vision of the world". For the Führer of this great Reich that was to last a thousand years, it was imperative to give Germany and its people, this Aryan race that was to dominate the surrounding sub-humans, the *Lebensraum*, the vital space necessary for its development. The conquest of new territories, preceded by the reconquest of lost territories, was the only path to the future that Hitler traced for the Germanic forces.

The first step was the annexation of Austria, the Anschluss, in March 1938. Shortly after, in September 1938, the Sudetenland was annexed, a part of Czechoslovakia populated by German families.

Then, Hitler invaded Poland on September 1, 1939, then France in June 1940 and Northern Europe, while subjecting England to murderous air attacks directed almost exclusively against the civilian populations of London and the major cities of southern Britain. In June 1941, Hitler launched Operation Barbarossa and attacked Russia; within a few months, the Wehrmacht was at the gates of Moscow.

The expansion stops here. The Nazi armies will never go any further.

The invaders were gradually pushed back to Berlin, but it took the Allies three years to achieve this result. Three long years of fighting.

Hitler's expansionist ambitions were also exported to the Far East. In December 1941, Japan attacked the United States with a surprise bombing of the American fleet assembled at Pearl Harbor in the Hawaiian Islands.

The whole world went to war. This is how Adolf Hitler's Third Reich and the Axis forces united behind it wanted it: sixty-one nations fought against each other in a deluge of iron, fire, blood and death. In all, more than sixty million people lost their lives in this conflict, the deadliest in human history. More than half of these victims were civilians, women, children and the elderly, annihilated by criminal ambitions that had nothing to do with them.

Such was the gigantic cost of the Munich renunciation in the face of Hitler in September 1938: the exorbitant and inhuman price of cowardice, compromise and naivety. For if, at that precise moment, the British and the French had had the courage to stand firm in the face of Hitler, who wanted to carve up Czechoslovakia, the history of the 20th century would have been profoundly different.

On the plane taking him back from Munich, on this day in September 1938, Édouard Daladier, "the bull of the Vaucluse", has nothing of the scolding politician whose stentorian voice covers the most vindictive heckles of the opposition in the French National Assembly. Since taking off from German soil, he has been brooding.

"Fooled! I've been fooled!" he grumbles.

His resentment was directed less at Hitler, whose intentions to annex part of Czechoslovakia were perfectly clear, than at Neville Chamberlain, the British Prime Minister. The Nazi dictator made no secret of the fact that he would send his troops to invade the Sudetenland, even if a war were to ensue. At least we knew where we stood. But Chamberlain! "He was a coward and a fraud, as the English know so well," Daladier ranted. From the rumors that reached his ears, Daladier understood that Chamberlain and his damned soul, Lord Halifax, had for a moment considered signing a separate agreement with the Germans that included the cession of a colony in Africa: presumably the Belgian Congo. Right across from the French Congo and its capital, Brazzaville! And without referring to the French government! "Where is the Franco-British alliance?" boiled the President of the Council!

Édouard Daladier understood perfectly the rationality of Hitler's strategy, his *Weltanschauung,* as he invoked it at every turn. Germany needed space, *Lebensraum,* to shelter and feed its population, and raw materials to feed its industry. It must therefore find them at all costs. So, for Hitler, the Sudetenland or the Belgian Congo would in any case only be a first step to reinforce the resources of the Great Reich.

Daladier wanted to stop these expansionist ambitions without delay. The French army was not ready, especially the air force, but the German army was even less ready!

Chamberlain and Halifax did not hear it that way. They spent hours pleading for appeasement, invoking the spirits of the

Entente Cordiale to obtain the Frenchman's assent. Daladier gave in. He signed the death warrant for Czechoslovakia, with no other counterpart than the Nazi dictator's word to stay put.

Daladier's plane has now left German territory. Two more hours of flight and it will approach Le Bourget airfield.

- What do you think, Bonnet?" asked Daladier to Georges Bonnet, the Minister of Foreign Affairs.

- We have saved the peace. The socialists will be satisfied, declares Georges Bonnet, fatalistic, with a tone that lacks conviction.

- I don't care about socialists! I'm talking about the French!

- I don't know. I have never understood the French. Nobody understands the French. They are the most incomprehensible people in the world," the minister calmly asserted.

- What about you, Leger? What is your opinion? Are they going to tear us apart?" Daladier asked Alexis Leger, the experienced diplomat who accompanied the French delegation.

- Mr. President," replied Alexis Leger, "we have fallen into a very French weakness with these Germans: pactomania. We love to sign pacts, the pact of this, the pact of that, the pact with some, the pact with others... Signing a pact clears us from not respecting what is inside this pact. The Germans have circumvented us thanks to our own weakness. We have no illusions about respecting this pact, and we signed it anyway. If the French realize that we have only applied a national strategy, they will not hold it against us. But of course, there is no one more fickle than the French. So let's expect to be led to the scaffold!

The diplomat concludes his tirade with a knowing smile. Alexis Leger, known as the poet of Saint-John Perse, is equal to himself: nebulous.

- Leger," interrupted Georges Bonnet, "you are a true Frenchman: perfectly incomprehensible!

Alexis Leger did not answer. He does not appreciate Georges Bonnet, this lawyer, an old hand in politics, who has occupied almost all the ministries in the course of his long career: crafts, public works, finance, budget, trade and now the Ministry of Foreign Affairs, at the head of which this anti-Semite has proposed to send two hundred thousand French Jews to the colonies. Bonnet was even Minister of the Post Office; he should have stayed there! thinks Leger. It is probably in this position that he could give the best of himself...

"They are going to split us up, that's for sure..." grumbles Daladier who, to end the discussion, turns sulkily towards the porthole.

The plane now turned around Le Bourget; it made a flawless approach. Through the window, Édouard Daladier saw a large crowd gathered around the terminal.

"Here, I was sure of it! They are here to lynch us! I hope Sarraut did what was necessary to protect us!"

Former governor of Indochina, Albert Sarraut was the Minister of the Interior, an old radical-socialist companion of Édouard Daladier, one succeeding the other on several occasions as President of the Council.

The plane lands. The crowd rushes and surrounds the plane, shouting, screaming slogans, raising their arms, making the plane restless.

- Let's go! makes Daladier. Courage! I go out first. I will talk to them. You will have time to escape. Go and find the troops!

The flight attendant opens the door. A huge clamor rises.

"Long live Daladier! Long live peace! Long live President Daladier!" shouted the enthusiastic crowd.

Édouard Daladier is one moment disconcerted. He turns to his companions, looking both frightened and desperate, and points to the jubilant crowd:

"Ah...the jerks!"

Carried in triumph by the crowd, Daladier moves away, a pout of sadness on his face. The French did not understand anything! The war is inevitable and they are not aware of it! If they knew...

That evening, Hjalmar Schacht returned to Gühlen in a dejected state. In the car, he did not exchange a word with the Reichsbank driver who drove him. The old financier looked at the landscape without really seeing it, his eyes lost in the void. Once in Gühlen, Schacht hardly noticed that he had arrived in front of his large house. The driver had to call out to him to bring him out of his torpor.

- Mr. President?

- Hummm?

- Mr. Chairman, we have arrived.

- Ah!...

Mechanically, the great financier gets out of the car. On the staircase, the housekeeper welcomes him, takes off his towel and his trench-coat.

- I'm going into the library. I don't want to be disturbed. I won't have dinner.

Hjalmar Schacht collapsed in his usual chair. He does not yet fully realize the extent of the catastrophe. His friend Erwin von Witzleben, the Wehrmacht general with whom he had meticulously prepared a plan to overthrow Hitler and take power, informed him that in Munich, against all odds, the French and British had signed an agreement authorizing Germany to annex the Sudetenland. There will be no war. Not for the moment. Hitler became a national hero.

Together with Erwin von Witzleben, Hjalmar Schacht had devised a plot to depose Hitler, but without killing him; the former Führer would have been tried. Schacht and the new government would have set up a government of national unity that would have been able to prepare for an easing of relations with the rest of Europe. For weeks they had been meeting with other men whom they suspected might be both good men and capable of some assistance in a particular action. To Schacht's surprise, a fair number of military men were convinced.

But it was a failure! Impossible to launch the coup: any action against Adolf Hitler and his henchmen would now be doomed to disaster.

The disaster is indeed here: the precision mechanism that should have driven the Nazis out of power and prevented the war has become a death trap for those who built it. And yet, war is coming. Hjalmar Schacht knew this: he had personally worked like hell to equip the Wehrmacht with the best weapons and make it the most powerful fighting force in Europe. And Adolf Hitler had every intention of using this strike force; he hardly hid the fact. Schacht thought that at least Daladier, the French President of the Council, was convinced of this. But he was not. By signing these agreements of shame which sacrificed Czechoslovakia, the French and the British did not prevent the war. They just made it inevitable, because from then on, driving Hitler out of power became impossible. And Hitler is war.

The war, the deaths, the dramas, the tears... Chaos was only delayed by a few months, and Hjalmar Schacht was aware of this: as a minister, he had access to privileged information that he knew how to interpret. After the Sudetenland, Hitler wanted to continue the expansion to the East.

A few months gained for a sure war. What a sadness!

In the quiet of his estate in Gühlen, Hjalmar Schacht also realized that he and his family were now in danger. The aborted plot was known to far too many people, especially the military. These people lived in isolation and talked a lot; who knew if one of them would betray them, or simply be indiscreet? Which members of the conspiracy should he be wary of?

Witzleben? There is nothing to fear from him; this general is a magnificent man, his whole being is devoted to the cause and in his personal behavior, he is as strict as a Jesuit and as talkative as a Carthusian monk. General Ludwig Beck? He is of an identical temperament. Even if they were denounced, they would never talk. Admiral Canaris, the head of the Abwehr, the military intelligence service, was too keen on secrecy to let the slightest information about the plot slip out. Hans Gisevius, with his experience as a diplomat and spy, was able to blend in and disappear in time if necessary. Ulrich von Hassel, another diplomat, is so clever that he can protect himself. But there are others in the conspiracy who are much more conspicuous. The old Prussian nobles, for example. Baron Kurt von Hammerstein, whom Schacht had contacted because of his connections in the military high command, was not always very discreet, being used to calling Nazis criminals in public; moreover, it was common knowledge that he helped the Jews. When, following the Nuremberg Laws, Jews were excluded from the Nobility Club, Hammerstein resigned with a bang and slammed the door. Kurt von Hammerstein's passionate personality was definitely not to be trusted. Karl Heinrich von Stülpnagel is more reassuring. A Prussian general, the son of a Prussian general, the great-grandson of a Prussian general, and having married the daughter of a Prussian general, this calm and level-headed aristocrat, a *Generalleutnant* at the Army General Staff, would know how to obtain information from reliable sources in order to find out if the plot was to be revealed. We can count on him. Halder and Brauchitsch? Schacht feared their indecision after meeting them, not that they would denounce the plot. These two soldiers had a deep sense of honor. And then there are those whom Schacht knows less about, but whom Witzleben recruited because he trusted them. General Erich Hoepner, for example, was nicknamed the Old Cavalier by his soldiers. Hjalmar Schacht met him once. With all his soul, Hoepner embraced the motto of experienced horsemen: "Forward, calm and straight!" The role that Witzleben had assigned him in the organization was crucial: General Hoepner, at the head of his troops, who adored him, as one adores a great leader, was to neutralize the SS stationed in Berlin. Hoepner was cut out for this challenge: reassuring, determined, authoritarian, his soldiers would have followed him as one man. Such a leader never betrays. Then there was Carl Goerdeler, the politician with a love of Christian values; if this inveterate talker held his tongue, it should be fine.

Thinking about it for a long time in the quiet of his library, Schacht is somewhat reassured. Because of the circumstances, the incredible naivety of the English and the fatal resignation of the French, the plot is dead. He has failed, his friends have failed, but these men with whom he had meticulously prepared the mechanics of the coup d'état are true companions, well chosen, devoted to the cause of Germany. If Schacht is right, their safety should not be threatened. Tomorrow Hjalmar Schacht will go to the Reichsbank, as usual. He will not run away. He must behave in a perfectly normal way; everyone's survival depends on it.

And if an arrest should happen... Well, *Schade!* He had misplaced his trust. For a financier, this is a crippling malpractice. His career and his life will be over and he will have deserved it. In economics, as in conjuring, you can't afford to be wrong.

In reality, the conspirators of the 1938 plot were not discovered. Most of them continued to participate in the resistance against Hitler. But at the end of the road, all of them lost their lives, except two: Hjalmar Schacht and Hans Gisevius, the spy-diplomat. The others ended their lives hanging from butcher's hooks or committing suicide, but much later, in 1944. Resisting Hitler required an extraordinary sense of sacrifice.

After the failure of the conspiracy, which was nipped in the bud by the indelible shame of Munich, Schacht was only remotely associated with the actions of the resistance: even though the financier had played an active role in 1938, he was distrusted. Despite his dismissal from the Ministry of Economics and from the presidency of the Reichsbank, Schacht remained a minister of state without portfolio. Schacht was still a full member of the Nazi governmental organization: he was still consulted by Hitler on certain economic matters, and sometimes he was offered to take over official functions, such as taking over the finances of occupied Belgium, as he had done in 1914. Schacht declined these offers, but for the resistance, it was difficult to rely on a person so closely linked to the regime in place. He was visited in Gühlen from time to time to see if he would be willing to participate in a government on the day Hitler and the Nazis were finally got rid of. Schacht, with the caution of a banker, answered elliptically. During the attempts on Hitler's life in 1943, Schacht was not told of the actions that were being planned, but his name was at the top of the list of conspirators for the formation of a government capable of regaining control of the country and making peace with the Allies. After 1943, Schacht's uncompromising character, which only envisaged the position of chancellor for himself after Hitler's death, pushed him further away from the resistance. Schacht, moreover, was particularly keen to avoid meetings with some of the pillars of the resistance, such as Carl Goerdeler, whose gossip and excessive agitation endangered those he contacted. On the other hand, the financier received a few officers in Gühlen, mainly friends of his son who was fighting on the Eastern Front. Occasionally, one of them would say a few words about operations against Hitler that were in preparation; Schacht would encourage them.

But without going any further: when the last conspiracy was launched, Operation Valkyrie by Colonel Count Claus von Stauffenberg, Hjalmar Schacht was kept completely out of it.

Morally, Schacht felt a certain guilt for having been the instrument of Hitler's success. Like the sorcerer's apprentice, Hjalmar Schacht, the great financier who believed he could control Adolf Hitler and guide him on the path to sensible government, had failed dramatically in this endeavor. On the contrary, it was he who was manipulated: during the first years of his reign, Hitler used his talents and then dismissed him when he wanted to.

Schacht was the creator of Hitler's power. Despite his entry into the resistance, he will not be the one to destroy it. He will be all the less so because his association with Hitler will have made him suspect in the eyes of those who want to act. His talents are recognized, but his compromises are known. Schacht had constituted himself as an auxiliary to an apprentice dictator in order to launch him onto the stage; it was difficult to count on him to know how to stop the Führer once his power was firmly consolidated. Schacht, the arrogant one, took this painful lesson. But many will also have learned this the hard way: protected by Satan and his demons, Adolf Hitler will have been invulnerable until his death.

Who could have stopped Adolf Hitler?

Not Hjalmar Schacht, whose 1938 plot ended before it began, scuttled by the French and British in Munich.

Not Georg Elser.

This communist, a cabinetmaker by profession, decided to act alone. Every year, Hitler celebrates the memory of his failed coup d'état of 1923 in a Munich brewery, the Bürgerbräukeller. Georg Elser decided to kill Hitler with a bomb placed in the brewery, which would explode while Hitler was giving his speech. A year of preparation was necessary. Every night for several weeks, Elser lets himself be locked up in a broom closet in the brewery, hidden behind the mops and coats of the cleaning ladies. When the establishment closes its doors to its last customer and the last cleaning lady has left, when the city is asleep and no more passers-by venture into the streets, Elser comes out of his hiding place and digs. He dug a cavity in a column, next to the place where Hitler's desk is still installed. A few days before the celebration, Elser placed a powerful bomb and a clockwork mechanism of rare precision that he had made himself into the cavity. But that evening, November 8, 1939, Adolf Hitler was in a hurry. He did not indulge in the great lyrical flights of fancy that he was accustomed to. His speech lasts forty minutes less than usual. When the bomb exploded, Hitler had already been gone for thirteen minutes. More than sixty people were injured, eight dead, but not Hitler. Elser is arrested; he spends the war in several concentration camps with a favorable regime. Hitler, for some reason that Elser never understood, kept him alive. He finally had him executed just before the Americans liberated the camp where Elser was then a prisoner, in Dachau.

Who to stop Adolf Hitler?

Not Henning von Tresckow.

Generalmajor of the Wehrmacht, he planned to kill Hitler by blowing up the plane carrying the dictator. In March 1943, he placed two bottles of cognac rigged with a bomb in the plane that was taking Hitler from Smolensk to Berlin. The detonator was set to trigger the infernal machine while the plane was in flight. However, the temperature is very low and blocks the device. The bomb did not explode and Hitler's plane landed safely at Tempelhof. Tresckow rushed to Berlin to retrieve the bottles of brandy and miraculously succeeded. The plot had not been hatched. Henning von Tresckow committed suicide one year and five months later, the day after the failure of Count Claus von Stauffenberg's Operation Valkyrie, in which he was involved. He was then commander of a unit on the Russian front. Tresckow blew himself up with a grenade in order to make it look like he was a victim of Soviet partisans and thus avoid prosecution of his family.

Who will stop Adolf Hitler?

Not Rudolf Christoph von Gersdorff.

Two weeks after Tresckow's attempt, this officer at the General Staff decided to kill Hitler, but also Himmler and Göring, during a visit of the Führer to the Berlin arsenal where he had to inaugurate an exhibition of weapons and uniforms taken from the Russians. Gersdorff placed two magnetic mines in his pockets. He is ready to commit a suicide bombing to end the life of the Nazi dictator. As Hitler approaches, Gersdorff isolates himself in the bathroom and, moving as quickly as he can, arms one of the two explosives. When he comes out, it is already too late. Adolf Hitler, in a very bad mood, has left after a brief visit to the exhibition. Gersdorff defuses the bomb in extremis. He later handed it over to Colonel Count von Stauffenberg, who used it in his own attempt. Gersdorff continued the war in Normandy, where he was a hero in the face of the Allied landing forces. He was one of the only conspirators against Hitler in the Wehrmacht to survive the war. He devoted the rest of his life to charity work and died in 1980 in Munich.

Who will stop Adolf Hitler?

Not Colonel Count Claus von Stauffenberg.

Author of the ultimate attempt to kill Hitler, he first leads a glorious career as an officer loyal to Nazism. He was wounded in the strafing of his car in North Africa and lost the use of one eye and several fingers. While he became an officer in the General Staff, he distanced himself from the Nazi party and Hitler, whom he believed should disappear for the sake of Germany. On July 20, 1944, he had to attend a meeting with Hitler at his headquarters in the *Wolfsschanze*, the "wolf's den" near Rastenburg in East Prussia; Stauffenberg placed a bomb in a briefcase and put it in the conference room at Hitler's feet. He then disappeared because he had to return to Berlin to direct the operations to take over power after the Führer's death. In his absence, one of the participants in the meeting accidentally moved the briefcase behind a leg of the table where the cards were laid out. This gesture saved Hitler. The bomb exploded, killing several people, but Hitler was only slightly injured. That same afternoon, he was able to go to the station to greet the Italian dictator Benito Mussolini who was visiting East Prussia. Stauffenberg, from a distance, saw the explosion. He is convinced that Hitler could not have survived it. He flies to Berlin where he spreads the news of Hitler's death. The information was spread to the main military leaders who, one after the other, rallied to the rebellion. But while Berlin and some military regions, including Paris, commanded by Karl Heinrich von Stülpnagel, who had been part of the Schacht conspiracy in 1938, began to tip in favor of the insurgents, the news that Hitler was not dead began to circulate. The fight changes its soul. The lukewarm, the followers, the undecided, in short, all those who had joined the insurgency out of opportunism, turned their backs and started to fight the rebellion. The insurgents are overwhelmed. One after the other, they surrendered; the regiments that had rallied to them returned to their barracks; the SS that the conspirators had captured and taken prisoner were freed. Order returned to Berlin and to the Greater Reich. Claus von Stauffenberg and the officers who had led the insurrection with him were shot the same evening.

Hitler's revenge will be terrible. Thousands of arrests, unbearable tortures, parodies of trials led by the judge Roland Freisler, a rabid and hysterical Nazi, and which systematically conclude with death sentences followed by hundreds of executions... The Nazi dictator is ruthless.

Of the conspirators in the Schacht plot of 1938, almost all were part of Operation Valkyrie in 1944. They would lose their lives. General Beck, who was to take power at the end of the Valkyrie plan, was allowed to commit suicide. He missed and was shot by a soldier. Carl Goerdeler was tortured for many months before being beheaded. Erwin von Witzleben was sentenced to death and hanged, as was Erich Hoepner, the Old Rider. Ulrich von Hassel, the elegant diplomat with a sharp intellect and strong Christian and humanist convictions, suffered the same fate; with his wit and sense of repartee, he had the luxury of ridiculing the people's court, the Volksgerichthof, during his appearance, before being taken to be hanged. Karl Heinrich von Stülpnagel was summoned to Berlin to explain his actions in Paris during the conspiracy: he had had 1,200 SS men arrested, and his superior, Hans Günther von Klüge, who had been tempted to join the Valkyrie, released them by betraying the conspiracy. Stülpnagel tried to commit suicide near the river Meuse, not far from Verdun, while taking a break with his driver. The general shot himself in the head and fell into the water. The driver dived in and saved Stülpnagel from drowning. Stülpnagel was taken to the hospital in Verdun and treated by doctors who managed to stabilize his wound, but he was still blind. Taken to Berlin, he was tried by Judge Freisler and sentenced to be hanged. To get him to the butcher's hook where a thin metal cord would slowly strangle him, the poor blind man, panting from the damage to his brain, had to be led by the hand, like a small child. Among the Wehrmacht officers who had helped Schacht in 1938, only one escaped the wrath of Hitler's vengeance: Kurt von Hammerstein, the Prussian baron who was revolted by the fate of the Jews. He had died a year earlier of cancer. If he had still been alive, there is no doubt that he would also have been part of Operation Valkyrie.

Of all the conspirators in 1938, four survived Valkyrie.

Two were active members of the Valkyrie: Hans Gisevius, the spy-diplomat, who managed to escape, and Admiral Canaris, who was arrested. Hitler spared him temporarily for a meticulous and cruel interrogation.

Two did not participate in Valkyrie: General Franz Halder, still hesitant, and Hjalmar Schacht. But both were nevertheless arrested by the Gestapo.

The Wehrmacht, which for years had provided the largest contingents of conspirators against Hitler, was decapitated and purged. Even Rommel, the hero of the war in Africa, was forced to commit suicide. From then on, the Wehrmacht lost all its influence to the SS, which became the sole masters in the conduct of the war.

As a final insult to the officers who had tried to kill him without succeeding, when Hitler finally disappeared nine months later, he owed it to himself, and to him alone. With the fierce determination that was his, while the Russians led the final assault on Berlin, he committed suicide by absorbing cyanide and simultaneously shooting himself in the head: no chance of escaping.

Very effective!

The same cannot be said for the Wehrmacht. Beyond that, one is even amazed at the catastrophic record of this elite army. Sixteen attacks against Hitler, all failed! How could such clumsy and unlucky people conquer all of Europe?

Of course, Hitler did not make their task any easier: unpredictable, changing his schedule a thousand times, suspicious as a fox, protected by a fanatical praetorian guard ready to die for him, Hitler was not easy to target. Moreover, he was served by an insolent luck, the luck of the devil, which allowed him to dodge these multiple assassination attempts. They were organized by officers who had made a brilliant career in the army, who had numerous feats of arms, and who were experienced in the use of weapons and explosives.

You can't blame them.

These men were heroes, endowed with an immense sense of honor and ready for most of them to sacrifice their lives. But to be a good conjurer, it is probably better to be an unscrupulous mercenary with a strong appetite for treason...

What should we conclude from this? For a plot to be organized effectively, it is better not to involve the military. Hjalmar Schacht should have known this. Businessmen, with whom honor is generally not present and who, on the other hand, cultivate with relish the ignorance of scruples and the taste for treachery, are much more efficient. The conspiracies organized by them have the best chances of success, especially when it is a question of overthrowing the power in a country.

In the post-war years, Schacht, who travelled the world, had a clear demonstration of this.

Jocobo Arbenz Guzmán was president of Guatemala in the 1950s, and the agrarian reform he initiated in 1952 was designed to return to the country's population the unused land that belonged to large foreign agricultural companies. As a landowner himself, he gave up a large part of his properties to the benefit of modest families. Arbenz's exemplary demonstration was not enough to convince the American multinational United Fruit to show the same generosity; the latter organized a coup d'état in 1954 and Arbenz was driven from power.

Elected in 1970, President Salvador Allende gave his country a socialist orientation with the nationalization of entire sectors of the economy and a redistribution of goods to the poorest. He was overthrown and assassinated in September 1973 in a coup organized by the American company ITT with the help of the CIA.

In Ecuador, Jaime Roldós Aguilera was elected president in 1979. In 1981, he had the Ecuadorian parliament pass a new law on hydrocarbons that limited the rights of American companies in the exploitation of oil. His plane crashed in May 1981 near the Peruvian border.

In the 1970s, Panamanian President Omar Torrijos had pursued a social policy that was very much oriented towards the people, with the redistribution of agricultural land, the creation of schools and jobs, and plans to put an end, with the help of Japanese investors, to the monopoly of American companies on the exploitation of the Panama Canal. He disappeared in a plane crash in July 1981, two months after his colleague Roldós from Ecuador.

Yes, the big international companies and businessmen excel in coups d'état.

The most famous assassination of heads of state in the 20th century may have been carried out by them. According to many investigators, the Mafia, which is only ever an organization of businessmen, albeit a special kind, probably ordered and organized the assassination of President John Fitzgerald Kennedy in Dallas on November 22, 1963. The shooters had perfect vantage points, unobstructed and unguarded by security forces, conveniently positioned at a distance, and left their victim no chance to escape. The assassin designated as the scapegoat, Lee Harvey Oswald, was arrested within hours of the crime and was himself shot dead two days later as he left the police station in handcuffs and defenseless. Thus his silence was guaranteed. Oswald was in the middle of a compact crowd of police officers. The police were so indifferent and passive during the execution that the question of their complicity is hardly in doubt. The executioner's name was Jack Ruby: a nightclub owner with ties to the mafia.

A perfectly oiled organization.

This is a highly efficient mechanism that Hjalmar Schacht, a fan of meticulously thought-out and determinedly executed projects, certainly appreciated as a connoisseur.

Kennedy didn't have a chance.

Not everyone can be called Adolf Hitler.

Chapter 9. The Prisoner

I spent three years in Gühlen, away from the governmental life of the Third Reich. I enjoyed the rest I could find there after a life of hard work. I was torn away from my thebaid in July 1944, when I was taken to prison. I was 67 years old, an advanced age for some. Not for me, my capacity for work and reflection was intact; but I must admit that on occasion, when I returned from long walks of several hours in and around my land, I felt tired.

Hitler had dismissed me as Minister without Portfolio in January 1943, after a gentle provocation on my part. Indeed, I had hardly any ministerial activity left, but due to an error of the government secretariat, I received at the end of 1942 a draft ordinance signed by Hermann Göring, which planned to withdraw students from secondary education to assign them to civil protection in airfields or public buildings. I was asked for my opinion on this text. I took the opportunity to express, in the clearest terms, my opposition to this project, as well as to ironically point out the many errors of appreciation of Hitler and Göring: I wrote a letter in which I insisted on the erroneous assertion that England would be put out of action by the Luftwaffe of the fat marshal, the lie according to which the

Russian resistance had been definitively broken, the impossibility of a landing of the Allies in North Africa, which had nevertheless occurred, and I thus continued my sarcasm for a few pages.

The reaction was not long in coming: Hitler dismissed me a month later from my position as minister. As for Göring, whose propensity to make a fool of himself was undeniable, he responded to the voice of his master, like a slavish lapdog, by expelling me from the Prussian State Council. When I read his letter, remembering that this important Council had not met for more than six years, I could not help but laugh. What a harsh punishment I was enduring!

I was thus freed from my ties to Hitler. Incidentally, I had not seen him since 1941, when I had come to tell him the news of my remarriage, as was fitting for a Reich minister. I was marrying a young woman of stunning beauty and remarkable culture; she was thirty years younger than I was. In her presence, I, who was naturally rather reserved and austere, revealed myself to be witty, outgoing, laughing and always ready to have fun! I think I had waited for this age that some people consider too old to discover love. My wife gave me two little girls, Constance and Cordula, who were the joy of my old age.

During this last meeting in February 1941, Hitler was icy cold with me. He did not congratulate me or compliment me on this happy event. Hitler had been mortified by the ridicule he had had to endure three years earlier at the wedding of my fellow War Minister, Werner von Blomberg. I was moderately fond of Blomberg; as an ardent admirer of Hitler, a kind word from the dictator would put him in a state of near ecstasy. In the opposite situation, he was unable to resist when Hitler raised his voice, so much so that the generals of the General Staff nicknamed him "the rubber lion". Blomberg had experienced a personal tragedy when his first wife, Charlotte, the mother of his five children, died in 1933. Four years later, he fell in love with a very young woman, Margarethe Gruhn, who was thirty-seven years younger than he was. When their marriage proposal was announced, Hitler exploded with joy:

- Wunderbar, *Blomberg! That's what I call German energy!*

- Mein Führer, *does the age difference not bother you?*

- *Blomberg, the Third Reich is the most modern nation in the world! Age difference? We must repudiate this snobbery from another era! You are marrying a young woman? I congratulate you. You will give the Reich new children! And do you know, Blomberg? I will be your best man at the wedding!*

- Mein Führer, *I am immensely honored...*

- *Perfectly!" interrupted Hitler. And if you wish, I will ask* Reichsmarschall *Göring to be the second witness! The entire Third Reich will bless your marriage!*

So it was done. Hitler and Göring, the witnesses to the union, went to the War Ministry, where the marriage was celebrated in some privacy. I remember that Blomberg could not hold back his tears when Hitler embraced him.

Two weeks later, a photograph began to circulate in the offices of the Chancellery and the Ministry of the Interior. It had been received at the Direction centrale de la police criminelle, accompanied by an anonymous letter. The photo showed a young woman, completely naked, wearing only a pearl necklace; on the back of the photo was written a name: Margarethe Gruhn. The investigation revealed that the young woman in question was a prostitute who had been arrested several times for soliciting on the public highway, and that the photo had been taken by a Jewish man who specialized in selling pornographic photos in busy places such as train stations and on Unter den Linden Boulevard.

When "well-meaning" hands circulated a copy of this photo to my office, I recognized Blomberg's young wife...

Frau von Blomberg was a prostitute! Who was photographed in obscene poses by a Jew! And Hitler had witnessed her wedding! The Führer was furious. He sacked Blomberg on the spot, who for once showed character in the face of Hitler by refusing to cancel his wedding. Poor old man! He was in love and found in this love the strength he had always lacked to resist Hitler. I think he went to Italy with his wife and returned to Germany a little later, after the war started, but I never heard from him again. May he have been happy with his Margarethe... Many years later, I learned incidentally that he had been arrested by the Allies at the end of the war and that he had died in a prison camp in Nuremberg. Perhaps I had unknowingly come across him during my own captivity.

My wife obviously had nothing in common with Blomberg. She had a degree in art history and philosophy and was employed at the Munich Art House. But my good fortune in falling in love with this woman and being loved by her opened my eyes to the judgment I had made of Blomberg at the time. I had been severe in my attitude toward Blomberg; like the others, I had laughed at his bad adventure and resented the disgrace that had befallen the government through his fault. I was in no condition to understand: I had not yet known love.

I had been all the more severe with Blomberg because Göring and Himmler, the head of the Gestapo, assisted by his evil mind Reinhard Heydrich, his sinister deputy, took advantage of his disgrace to launch a terrible plot. Göring wanted to discredit Blomberg's deputy, Werner von Fritsch, at all costs. Rumors of his homosexuality had spread around 1933, shortly after Hitler's arrival in power and the formation of the first government in which Fritsch was already Blomberg's deputy. Hitler refused to believe it at the time. But after the affair of the marriage of the Minister of War with a prostitute, Hitler demanded that Fritsch's file be brought out. Hermann Göring feared Fritsch, whom he saw as a competitor for the post of War Minister, which he coveted now that Blomberg had been sacked. To get into Göring's good graces, Himmler decided to extract a notorious homosexual, thief and blackmailer from the concentration camp where he was being held. This perverse individual declared that he formally recognized Fritsch as one of his lovers. Hitler's anger knew no bounds. A week after Blomberg's dismissal, Fritsch was asked to leave his post. Göring's hands were now free and Himmler, by discrediting the Wehrmacht's high command, further strengthened the power of the SS.

For my part, I had refused to believe in this story of a corneculus that had arisen so opportunely for Göring just after the Blomberg affair. I knew Fritsch well: a good man, upright, loyal, with a firm and balanced word. He fiercely denied the accusations. Considering the personalities of the accuser and the accused, a homosexual delinquent who earned his living through drugs and blackmail on the one hand, and a great soldier with unyielding loyalty on the other, it seemed to me that Fritsch should be believed.

Hitler preferred to chase him away.

A few months later, a thorough investigation showed that the whole affair was a machination. Göring then showed his true nature: with a duplicity of a rare hypocrisy, he who had set up this false accusation with Himmler obtained to preside over the military tribunal which rehabilitated Fritsch! Making an outrageous use of his acting talent, he vehemently protested against the lies that had plagued this magnificent soldier. Great! It was not to be believed!

When I think back to the snake's nest that was Adolf Hitler's environment, I regret that I was forced to leave it as a victim of

Hermann Göring's machinations. Yet this man had long claimed to be my friend.

Thanks to my wonderful wife, the years of retirement in Gühlen were like a dream. During my long walks in the countryside, I spent hours observing the birds, the deer herds, the ever-changing nature. I experienced a different life from that of business, of offices overloaded with files and meetings with the powerful leaders and financiers of this planet.

The peace lasted until July 20, 1944. Three days before, Berlin had been shaken by the revolt led by Stauffenberg, which ended in a bloodbath. While these events were taking place in the capital, I remember being in the Grunewald forest, just above Munich, watching wild boars fighting for dominance of their herd. The air was fine, a light mist hung between the trees, and except for the grunts of the male boars as they fought each other, a beautiful silence surrounded me; a beautiful and peaceful day, as one knows them in the countryside. After my mountain hike, a dinner cooked by the women in my life was waiting for me at my daughter's house; we were visiting her in Bavaria. Except for my son Jens, who was fighting on the Eastern front against the Russian armies, all my children were gathered around my wife and me. The family meal turned out to be frugal, as the restrictions hit us hard, like other Germans. But this moment of happy bliss of a loving family was for each of us a pure happiness. The older children were smiling and talking, the younger ones were playing hide-and-seek all around. We will never forget this evening of normal life of a united German family; a simple and harmonious evening as all should be.

Back in Gühlen on the morning of July 23, I was still in my night clothes when the cook knocked on our bedroom door. She told me that the criminal police wanted to see me. Through the window I saw that about ten cars were parked in the yard.

I went down to the living room.
Six policemen were there.
They informed me that I was under arrest.

On the night of July 23, 1944, in front of the Bendlerblock, the headquarters of the Wehrmacht in Berlin, Otto Skorzeny and Otto Ernst Remer were having a peaceful discussion. A little further on, in the courtyard of the building, which was violently lit by flak projectors, four bodies, still warm, were waiting to be loaded onto a truck. A military vehicle arrives and maneuvers to back up to the wall at the foot of which the bodies are slumped. One after the other, the soldiers load the dead into the truck in a jumble. First General Friedrich Olbricht, then *Oberleutnant* Werner von Haeften, then Colonel Albrecht Mertz von Quirnheim, and finally Colonel Count von Stauffenberg. The truck drove away while Skorzeny and Remer smoked their cigarettes.

Remer is the hero of the day. Thanks to him, the plot meticulously prepared by Claus von Stauffenberg has failed. Felonious officers wanted to kill Hitler, overthrow the Nazi regime and take power. They probably wanted to make peace with the Allies afterwards. But they failed and are now only corpses.

Otto Ernst Remer was the grain of sand that seized the beautiful mechanism. The conspirators tried to manipulate him: they made him believe that Hitler was dead and at the head of his regiment, they charged him with going to arrest the little doctor Goebbels, the minister of Propaganda. But Goebbels didn't let this happen; bravely, he confronted Remer and turned him around. The propaganda master managed to convince Remer, a very loyal Nazi, that Hitler was not dead. He even put him in telephone contact with the Führer. Otto Ernst Remer then committed his troops against the conspirators; he led the assault on the Bendlerblock, the army headquarters that the conspirators had taken over. The men of Valkyrie could not defend themselves for long. Moreover, the news that Hitler had survived the explosion that had ravaged his headquarters in the *Wolfsschanze* had quickly spread throughout the Wehrmacht. Those who, for a moment, had rallied to the coup d'état, had hurriedly returned to their barracks. The insurgents had received no reinforcements and had been captured by Remer and his men, whom the SS commanded by the famous Otto Skorzeny, the Nazi hero of the rescue of Mussolini, had come to support.

General Friedrich Fromm, the commander-in-chief of the reserve army, rushed to have the four Valkyrie leaders shot. Remer wanted to keep them alive, in accordance with the orders he had received from Goebbels. But Fromm overruled him.

- Hitler will not be happy, says Otto Skorzeny. He would certainly have liked to judge these traitors!

- You can't reason with Fromm," Remer replies. This guy is weird. He looked like he had something to be ashamed of.

- Perhaps. He was in too much of a hurry to eliminate Stauffenberg and his henchmen to have anything on his conscience. We'll investigate. Has Hitler spoken to you?

- Yes, at Minister Goebbels' house.

- So what?" asks Skorzeny.

- He wanted them alive. He wanted arrests. Many arrests. The Führer is right! We must clean up these vermin who are destroying the Reich from within!

- *Jawohl!*" agrees Skorzeny. I believe that in the days to come, we will not lack activity! Starting with him!" he concludes by pointing to General Fromm who passes in front of them, with a shifty look.

As Remer and Skorzeny had predicted, General Fromm, whose attitude during the Valkyrie had been so ambiguous, was arrested a few months later, then locked up in a concentration camp before being tried and sentenced to be hanged for cowardice in the face of the enemy. Hitler, sympathetic, commuted his sentence to being shot; the Nazi dictator was that day accessible to a certain form of pity.

In the days following Valkyrie, the SS, the Gestapo and the Reich Criminal Police increased the number of arrests in response to Hitler's fury. Five thousand people were rounded up in the Plötzensee prison in the Charlottenburg district of eastern Berlin or in the concentration camps nearby.

One of these five thousand was Hjalmar Schacht: on July 23, 1944, three days after the Valkyrie plot, to which he was a complete stranger, Schacht was arrested in the early hours of the morning at his estate in Gühlen.

Hitler wanted to decapitate all forms of opposition. The entire police force of the Great Reich was mobilized in this generalized manhunt on German territory. Hitler should have other concerns, however, because the Reich was cracking on all sides: in Italy, the Allies had reconquered the peninsula as far as Rome, whose enthusiastic population had welcomed them with jubilation. In the east, the Russians were in front of Warsaw and were pushing the German armies, unable to stabilize the front line, more and more. In the west, the American, British and French forces had gained a solid foothold in Normandy and were marching on Paris, which was liberated four weeks later. But for Hitler, who was losing touch with reality, the catastrophic military situation did not matter. All means must be mobilized to crush those who dared to plot against the Führer! Let the traitors who dared to raise their voice one day be thrown into prison! And eliminated! Hanged on a butcher's hook!

Himmler, who led the repression, had no proof of Hjalmar Schacht's involvement in the Valkyrie conspiracy, but it did not matter to him: he had the opportunity to make Schacht swallow his arrogance, this arrogant character who lectured him in the Council of Ministers with his unbearable condescension about finance. The punishment of the Valkyrie conspirators was to make the former Minister of Economics and ex-president of the Reichsbank, who had dared to criticize the dictator of the Third Reich for several years, disappear from the scene for good. Hitler approved of the arrest: he had not forgotten the episode of the ironic letter that mocked his errors of judgment. But the dictator still had some scruples about the great financier to whom he was so indebted: Hjalmar Schacht must therefore be treated correctly. An eventual execution would have to be approved by him beforehand, unless the investigation showed that the old banker was involved in the attack; in this case, let the merciless Nazi justice system take its course! The butcher's hook!

In the early morning, the Gühlen estate was completely sealed off: there was no way that Hjalmar Schacht could slip through the net. A full-scale military operation was mounted to prevent the old man from escaping, and he did not even think about escaping for a moment. Schacht allowed himself to be taken away by the disproportionately large police force that had been dispatched to seize him.

As the car in which he was seated drove across the Prussian plains, so peaceful under the summer sun, Hjalmar Schacht probably did not imagine that he would not be completely free until many years later, in 1951.

He was taken to the Ravensbrück concentration camp, eighty kilometers north of Berlin.

Ravensbrück, in the Nazi concentration camp system, was above all a camp designed to imprison and kill women and children; one hundred and thirty-two thousand of them were imprisoned there. Ninety thousand of them were mercilessly exterminated in this hell.

Upon his arrival, Hjalmar Schacht was locked in a cell in the annexed camp, the men's camp. He was held incommunicado, isolated from the other prisoners. No one came to question him for a few days. During the weekly shower he was allowed, he saw some of his fellow prisoners: General Halder, the undecided of his 1938 plot, was there, as well as some centrist politicians, university professors he vaguely recognized, and a cabaret actress, Isa Vermehren, whom he had had the opportunity to applaud in Berlin. A strange gathering of disparate individuals, lost in this camp, as if they had fallen by chance from another planet, and who all seemed dazed to find themselves prisoners of Adolf Hitler. A few days earlier, despite their more or less strong opposition to the Nazi regime, they enjoyed the privilege of living free in a Germany still spared by the war. The summer of 1944 looked bright, until the day the Gestapo came knocking at the door...

Hjalmar Schacht gets to know the sad existence of the prisoners: stripped of his civilian clothes, dressed in drugs that make you look like a convict to the point of transmitting his state of mind, only an immense effort of will can avoid feeling guilty all the time.

Daily life was punctuated by starvation meals, the chore of cleaning toilets and interrogations.

We wait.

The next day, we wait.

The day after, we are still waiting.

And so on. We wait.

Hjalmar Schacht distracted the hours with cockroach hunting. Fortunately, the game is plentiful; under the mattress, on the floor, on the walls, the cockroach tribe competes for territory with the hordes of bedbugs. The fight against the vermin is made difficult by the pissy brown color of the walls that surround the narrow universe of the old banker. The dirtiness of the decor allows the insects to blend in with the landscape, making the hunt interesting...

After a few days, the interrogations began. First of all, Schacht was taken to the nearby camp of Drogen. Despite the threats, Schacht said nothing but general things about himself or his loyal Nazi beliefs.

Then the treatment became less courteous. Hjalmar Schacht was transported to Berlin, to the cellars of the Security Headquarters on Prinz-Albrechtstraße. As an appetizer, Schacht was kept in solitary confinement in an underground dungeon; he did not see the light of day for four months. Four long months without the fresh air of the outside world; difficult for an old man to bear. The interrogations became rougher, but Schacht was not physically abused. Apparently, no one seriously thought that he had been involved in the attempt on Hitler's life, nor in any previous conspiracy; but he was questioned about his relatives, his relations, about conversations he had had with some or others, at political meetings or during business appointments. Did they talk about the fall of Hitler? About a future government? Who was present?

During these long weeks, Schacht only had contact with his jailers and the investigators.

In the washrooms, or during the bomb scares when he was led with the other prisoners into a narrow underground corridor, he could catch a glimpse of some of his fellow prisoners. Several of them had been his accomplices in the abortive coup d'état of

1938, and as far as they were concerned, they all participated in Valkyrie. Among those resistance fighters who persevered in the conspiracies, Schacht recognizes Carl Goerdeler, in a sad physical and moral state, and Wilhelm Canaris, the admiral, former head of the Abwehr, who also seems to have been severely beaten. He also identified Fabian von Schlabrendorff, a lawyer who had become an officer in the Wehrmacht, and Caesar von Hofacker, a cousin of Claus von Stauffenberg. But soon the latter no longer appeared: he was executed on December 20. General Fromm was there for a few weeks, as well as Herbert Göring, Hermann Göring's cousin. Schacht liked this pleasant and sympathetic businessman, an opponent of Hitler and of Hermann Göring, his perverse cousin whom he had hated for years; conversing with Herbert Göring, a cultured man full of finesse, was a pleasure. But in the Prinz-Albrechtstraße prison, silence reigned. Even during air raids, the slightest whisper is met with blows.

On February 3, 1945, as Berlin suffered one of the worst bombings of the war, Schacht was transferred with other prisoners to an unknown destination. The cell car drove through a city ravaged by flames. The Prinz-Albrechtstraße prison itself was partially destroyed: the cellars remained, but part of the superstructure was in flames when Schacht was evacuated. Entire streets were devastated and only smoldering sections of wall remained. The van had to make detours through the fires and rubble to get out of the city and to the police depot in Potsdam. There, the prison that served as a fallback for several Berlin detention facilities was overcrowded: Schacht had to share a cell with two companions, a former secretary of state whom he did not know well, and General Alexander von Falkenhausen with whom he had once been in contact: a former military governor of occupied Belgium, he was a friend of Witzleben's and knew about the 1938 plot, which he supported.

After the months of confinement and solitude on Prinz-Albrechtstraße, the brief stay in Potsdam prison brought some relief: the prisoners could walk freely in the prison yard and talk to each other. But soon a rumor spread: Hitler had given the order to execute all political prisoners. Suddenly, everything changed: the guards became aggressive again, they started barking wildly at the inmates, and there was no question of walking in the courtyard in semi-freedom. The prisoners are returned to their cells without mercy.

What's going on?

Hitler's orders?

Will the prisoners be executed?

After a few hours of calm, sounds of boots and keys are heard in the corridor. One unlocks. The door of the cell opens brutally.

- Schacht? Come on! *Schnell*!

Guards came and seized Hjalmar Schacht and threw him roughly into a car. Four SS men surrounded him.

- Where are we going?" asks Schacht.

- Quiet!

The car takes the road to Berlin. Schacht can see the ruined city, women, children and old people wandering around in search of water or food. These dusty, indifferent shadows pay no attention to the police car that drives around obstacles, piles of rubble and carcasses. Schacht shudders. Isn't that the direction of Prinz-Albrechtstraße that the car is taking? And if they bring him back there, it is to execute him...

Indeed, the car enters Prinz-Albrechtstraße. Schacht barely recognizes the area; there is almost nothing left of the sinister prison. The car stops in front of piles of rubble. Hjalmar Schacht felt the chill of death come over him as he was led towards what remained of the fortress building. Not much, really: a few rooms are still standing, at most. But the cellars with the gaols are intact. We go down one staircase, then another. Schacht recognized the long, familiar corridor. A cell is opened for him, an SS man removes his handcuffs, and the door is closed with a loud bang.

The silent and sinister solitude settles down again.

A few hours later, Schacht was taken from the cell. Hanging? The butcher's hook? Schacht lets himself be taken away. What else is there to do? A corridor, another one, a staircase...

No, this is not the execution room.

He was led into the courtyard, to the latrines dug in what appeared to be the remains of a shell hole. A board was installed so that one could sit down. Schacht is invited to relieve himself. A man is already there, with his pants down, busy defecating. Schacht recognizes him: it is Pastor Dietrich Bonhoeffer, one of the most generous and learned good men he has ever met in his life. In fact, this theologian has always demonstrated, through his simplicity, kindness and example, that he was a saint come down to earth. Schacht drops his pants and sits down next to him. The pastor's face is swollen, his forehead is bruised, his teeth are broken and his nose is deformed from the beating. But he smiles at Schacht and his eyes express an immense inner peace.

- How are you, Hjalmar?" he asks gently.

- I guess this is the end, my dear Dietrich. The end of what, I don't know exactly, but the end of something.

- The end or the beginning, who can be sure? answers the pastor. God has us in his holy custody. He watches over us. And even over them," Bonhoeffer added, pointing to the SS men who were watching them while smoking a cigarette. They will need it.

- I wish I had your confidence, Dietrich.

- Any news from your family? How are Constance and Cordula? The smiles on these little ones' faces were a great comfort.

- Nothing for months. I don't know anything about their fate.

The guards are approaching. It is time to finish and get dressed. Schacht never saw Bonhoeffer again. He was executed by hanging two months later in Flossenbürg.

The next day, two SS men came to get the old banker from his cell. Schacht once again expected the worst.

But no.

He was put on a bus with other prisoners: General Oster and Theodor Strünck, both former members of the Abwehr, the military intelligence service, General Thomas, former head of the war economy and armaments service, General Halder, the eternal indecisive, and the former Austrian Chancellor Schuschnigg with his wife and little daughter. The SS guards got on and the bus started. Direction, the southern freeway; the freeway he financed during his first year in Hitler's service, Schacht thought ironically.

The hours pass, quite quietly. The bus continues south, on the marvelous network of highways that was to make Germany prosperous and on which it passes almost exclusively military vehicles.

The night falls.

Midnight.

The bus stops.

A gate. Barbed wire. Watchtowers.

The vehicle stops in a courtyard where a battalion of soldiers armed with machine guns is waiting. The prisoners disembark. The air is cold, a crisp air from the surrounding Bavarian mountains.

They arrived; all around them was the Flossenbürg camp. Schacht knew this place by reputation: a large Messerschmitt aircraft factory was located nearby and employed prisoners in forced labor. The Reichsbank financed Messerschmitt, just as it financed other industrialists such as Krupp or Flick. The former president of the Reichsbank was therefore well aware of what was going on here. He knows that Flossenbürg was originally a labor camp, but rumor has it that it has now become an extermination camp.

- You don't get out of here alive!" mutters Schacht.

The prisoners are roughly taken to the cells. Schacht curled up in a corner and tried to sleep despite the freezing February temperature. Shouts and gunshots are heard.

What is going on in this camp?

These disturbing noises continue throughout the night.

Finally, in the morning.

Schacht is taken from his cell. A guard barks out:

"Twenty minutes! You get a twenty minute walk! *Los!*"

Hjalmar Schacht begins to walk, alone in the yard. He understands that he is once again in solitary confinement. In the distance, he sees convoys of men carrying stretchers covered with blankets. Obviously, they were carrying corpses. Sometimes you can see an arm or a leg hanging out from under the short blankets. The carriers move away towards the forest.

Where are they going?

It doesn't matter, after all. Schacht is in no doubt as to how he will get out of here: on one of these stretchers.

"Ende! Kommen Sie zurück!" barks the guard.

Twenty minutes have passed.

It's so quick, twenty minutes of breathing clean air.

End of the walk.

Schacht is taken back to his cell.

Back to isolation.

Impenetrable solitude.

This regime lasted several weeks. Schacht was neither interrogated nor mistreated. The only break in the routine was the sudden visit of the camp commandant, who violently opened the cell door one morning:

- Do you recognize me?" he shouts.

Yes, Schacht recognizes this. It was one of the police officers who had interrogated him in Berlin. The old banker remembers that he had exasperated this policeman with his arrogance and his contemptuous answers. The olibrius thus became the commander of this nightmare place; he now wore the SS uniform of *Sturmbannführer*. Hjalmar Schacht now has only certainty about his fate. He would not survive Flossenbürg.

Two months passed in solitary confinement. One thought never left Hjalmar Schacht's mind: his two little girls; the last time he saw them, they were two and a half and 15 months old. If they are still alive, Constance is now over 3 years old, and Cordula is over 2 years old.

But are they still of this world?

And where did they fail?

These questions are an obsession.

All the nights, all those days in silence.

Always the same questions.

Days follow days. Until the beginning of April: the days are then warmer even if the nights remain fresh.

One morning, there is a muted commotion in the camp.

The Americans are approaching.

Important prisoners must be evacuated.

Schacht was put on a bus, flanked by Generals Halder and Thomas, and Chancellor Schuschnigg, still accompanied by his wife and daughter. And the other participants in the trip from Berlin, Oster and Strünck?

No, no news.

They are not there.

Schacht would later learn of their execution by hanging, the same morning he left Flossenbürg. They were executed at the same time as Pastor Dietrich Bonhoeffer, the theologian whom Schacht had met in the latrines of the Prinz-Albrechtstraße prison. Schacht had no idea that the brave clergyman could be in the same camp as him.

On the way, the bus stops at other camps where personalities join the prisoners of Flossenbürg: General von Falkenhausen, and then a Russian, who turns out to be a nephew of Molotov, Stalin's minister, but also many others, so that the bus is soon overcrowded. Finally, in the evening, the bus arrives at the Dachau concentration camp.

In the Nazi concentration camp universe, Dachau was not an extermination camp, but a labor camp. On its porch is the famous maxim *Arbeit macht frei*, "work makes you free"; however, of the two hundred thousand prisoners who passed through this camp, the first of its kind created by the Nazis, thirty thousand perished from hunger, disease, mistreatment or were executed.

The "prisoners of distinction" were welcomed with a certain kindness: most of the SS had fled and the guards who remained in Dachau, in the special prisoners' section, were generally Wehrmacht soldiers: war wounded stranded there, because they were unusable on the front, and more concerned with buying themselves a few certificates of good conduct than with continuing the Nazi regime's work of death. Schacht spent a fortnight in Dachau, where he met up with personalities he knew well, such as Fritz Thyssen, the Nazi industrialist who did not hate the Jews, and the French politician Léon Blum. After Flossenbürg, despite the promiscuity and the food that barely prevented him from dying of hunger, the stay was almost pleasant for Schacht because he was no longer in isolation.

Then another evacuation, this time to the Reichenau camp, a few kilometers from Munich, and finally to Niederndorf, in the mountains of Tyrol.

There, obviously, the guards do not know what to do. They wait. They are rather friendly, they do not bully their prisoners anymore. Sometimes they even risk a courteous word. There is no longer any question of executions, torture or punishment. They are waiting for something. They are waiting for an event. But they don't know exactly what. They are waiting, that's all.

Finally, one morning in April 1945, the long-awaited event took place: an American soldier arrived at the camp gates.

He asks to see the commander.

This one goes out, he extends a hand to the American.

The GI turns on his heels without even looking at him and waves to his comrades, "Onward!"

The column of Yankee jeeps enters the camp.

It's over.

Hjalmar Schacht escaped death.

He can't believe it himself.

For most of the companions he had met or just glimpsed during the ten months he was plunged into the Styx of Hitler's death, the outcome was not so happy.

Many of the German resistance fighters arrested after Valkyrie ended up in Plötzensee prison. In this sinister building, nearly three thousand prisoners were executed, first by beheading with an axe, then by guillotine, and finally, when it was necessary to speed up the pace and satisfy Hitler's need for cruelty, by hanging. In the execution room, a metal bar with five butcher's hooks was installed. The condemned were tied up, the executioner passed a thin cord around their neck, usually made of metal, and the victim was hung; death by strangulation took several minutes of inhuman suffering. Sometimes, for those convicts for whom Hitler and his henchmen wanted extra refinement, the unfortunate ones were hanged once, so that they could experience the "taste of death," and then they were hung just before they expired. Then they were hanged a second time, until they died.

Carl Goerdeler, the talkative politician, Erwin von Witzleben, the inflexible military man and organizer of the 1938 conspiracy, Erich Hoepner, the Old Cavalier, Caesar von Hofacker, Stauffenberg's cousin, Karl Heinrich von Stülpnagel, the commander of Paris, Ulrich von Hassel, the learned diplomat, and most of the condemned prisoners of Operation Valkyrie, were executed at Plötzensee. One of them escaped this fate by one of those pirouettes of fate that life sometimes has the secret of. Fabian von Schlabrendorff was on trial before the Volksgerichthof, the people's court, of which the dreadful Roland Freisler was president. Freisler had already sentenced to death and had the main soldiers of the Wehrmacht executed when Schlabrendorff appeared before him. As luck would have it, the Allies chose this day for the umpteenth bombing of Berlin. The Volksgerichthof was destroyed. Judge Freisler was wounded and died shortly afterwards. Fabian von Schlabrendorff escaped conviction because of this "unfortunate" setback. He was also wounded during the bombing, recovered, was imprisoned in a concentration camp, and survived the war.

He became one of the leading judges of the Constitutional Court of the Federal Republic of Germany.

A miraculous fantasy of fate in the midst of tragedy.

Hitler also sometimes had similar fantasies with his prisoners, whom he played with as if they were toys.

Georg Elser, the cabinetmaker who was responsible for the Munich bombing in 1939, became a "special prisoner" of Hitler. After his capture, he was imprisoned in Berlin. When the city began to be bombed, Hitler had him imprisoned in the Oranienburg concentration camp, then in Dachau, but with the recommendation that he be treated well in both cases. Hitler wanted to keep him at his disposal in order to stage, when the time came, a show trial against communism and its murderous conspirators. The war prevents this beautiful project and Elser goes through it, from camp to prison, in rather comfortable conditions. Georg Elser, this communist worker, this ordinary and modest man who wanted, all by himself, to put an end to Hitler's dictatorship, was finally executed in Dachau on April 9, 1945, the day Hjalmar Schacht arrived in this same camp, and only a few days before the arrival of the American forces.

Another "special prisoner" was Herschel Grynszpan. This young Polish Jew murdered a German embassy attaché, Ernst vom Rath, in Paris on November 7, 1938. Joseph Goebbels used this murder as a pretext to unleash the "Kristallnacht" against the Jews of Germany. The trial of the young Jewish murderer in the French courts never took place because of the outbreak of war against the Third Reich. Grynszpan spent almost two years in preventive prison in France before the Germans were able to catch up with the convoy of prisoners in which he was held: as the German armies advanced, the prisoners were evacuated from prison to prison, always further south. Transferred to Germany, Herschel Grynszpan was locked up in the Sachsenhausen camp, where he was given preferential treatment for several years. He was finally executed at an undetermined date, probably at the end of 1944 or the beginning of 1945.

But the most emblematic case is that of Admiral Canaris.

With a remarkable intelligence, gifted for everything, especially for languages - he spoke five fluently - this promising naval officer was asked in 1923 by Colonel von Schleicher, the future chancellor of Germany who preceded Hitler to power, to create an intelligence service within the army. This was to be the Abwehr, the famous "fifth column". Nicknamed the Old Man because of his hair, which turned completely white at the age of 40, Canaris, intellectually brilliant, casual and cosmopolitan, extended his networks throughout Europe. He did not associate much with the Nazis, as he did not share their taste for drinking and orgies. A rather solitary but worldly man, he had many acquaintances, including Hjalmar Schacht, whom he held in high esteem. On the other hand, he had few friends, but very loyal ones, among them the Spanish general Franco. Canaris, like Schacht, disapproved of the persecution of the Jews and distrusted the Nazi party, which he considered harmful to Europe and Germany.

From 1938 onwards, Admiral Canaris plotted to oust Hitler from power, joining forces with Schacht in the attempted coup of 1938. After this failure, he began an extremely dangerous double or even triple game, informing the Allies of the imminent attack on France or the Soviet Union, sending a complete file on the extermination of the Jews to the Vatican, while gathering strategic information for Hitler on the Allied armies and setting up a very effective service in France to fight the resistance, which caused thousands of deaths.

During this time, against all caution, he took insane risks by personally saving many Jews.

Hitler's spy has a conscience; the mad dictator could not have imagined this.

The great leaders of the Gestapo and the SS, Himmler and Heydrich, whom he had known as a young man, when all three served on the same Kriegsmarine corvette, finally realized that the admiral was betraying the regime. From then on, he was lost. Canaris was arrested after Operation Valkyrie, and the elegant intellectual, a tennis and horse-riding enthusiast, began his descent into hell. Locked up with Hjalmar Schacht in the Prinz-Albrechtstraße prison, he was interrogated, humiliated, harassed and physically tortured.

But he doesn't talk.

On the contrary, this master manipulator manages to fool his torturers, extracting from them without their noticing information about the near end of the regime and the advance of the Russians and the allied forces.

In vain.

After the destruction of the Prinz-Albrechtstraße prison during the bombing in February 1945, Wilhelm Canaris was transferred first to the Buchenwald extermination camp and then to Flossenbürg, where Schacht saw him from a distance; the little admiral's figure had lost none of its distinction despite the convict's clothes, and his legendary white hair was recognizable from a distance. On the day Hjalmar Schacht left for Dachau, Wilhelm Canaris was hanged in Flossenbürg, together with his former collaborators Oster and Strünck, and the unfortunate pastor Bonhoeffer.

Hitler wanted special treatment for the admiral.

For the man who has deceived him so well for years, the dictator has planned a death whose atrocity is beyond imagination.

First of all, the executioner sticks a butcher's hook into his ribs and the victim is thus hanged by the abdomen. Then comes the actual hanging, but with the refinement of the "taste of death": first hung once by a thin cord that strangles him to the brink of death, the admiral is hung while he is dying. Then, the executioner hangs him again.

Wilhelm Canaris finally expires.

In the distance, the detonations of the American army's cannons can be heard, which will liberate the Flossenbürg camp ten days later.

Ten days too late for this devious but fair man. He believed that his intelligence would always allow him to get away with it in the midst of Nazi thugs, and he was wrong. Wilhelm Canaris' loyal friends did not forget the elegant little white-haired admiral: the caudillo Franco, who became dictator of Spain, took in Canaris' wife and two daughters after the war. The Jews did not forget him either: voices were raised to include Wilhelm Canaris, Hitler's spy, in the list of the Righteous. But the good deeds of this multi-faceted hero remain largely unacknowledged.

Hjalmar Schacht, Georg Elser, Herschel Grynszpan, Wilhelm Canaris: four of Hitler's "special prisoners. Hjalmar Schacht was the only one of the four to survive his stay in Hitler's prisons and camps.

However, Adolf Hitler had given clear orders.

Schacht was to be put to death before the liberation of the camps.

The old financier should not have survived.

The orders were not carried out.

No one, including Schacht himself, has ever understood why.

Chapter 10. The criminal

It quickly became clear to me that the Americans wanted to make an example of me and condemn me as a criminal.

At first, after our liberation, they were particularly kind. My companions and I thought that we would soon be reunited with our families and our lives and that we would be able to help rebuild Germany. After all, we had been opponents of Hitler and had only escaped death by a miracle.

The Americans evacuated us first to the mountain resort of Wildsee where they put us up in a hotel. After months in solitary confinement in a vermin-infested cell with no one to talk to, the walks along the mountain paths, through the forests that were bursting with spring freshness, were a permanent ecstasy. In the evening, we talked in the hotel lobby, without guards to torment us and bark absurd orders in our ears. On the contrary, we had the great Isa Vermehren, that wonderful singer and actress who was so famous in Berlin before the war, as a fellow inmate. She charmed us with her Viennese songs and the melodies we loved so much when peace reigned. Few of us could hold back our tears when she sang Lili Marleen, which was sung in chorus by the American and British soldiers who came to attend these impromptu recitals. I saw Isa Vermehren again much later, on television: she had entered the Congregation of the Heart of Jesus and had become a spiritual reference for a whole generation.

After a few days of this vacation, we were evacuated to Italy, to Verona, where we could stroll through the streets of this magnificent city. We found our taste for freedom, for friendly contacts with Italians, for the normal, quiet life of ordinary people. However, we suffered from the impossibility of contacting our families. In this Europe, which had only just come out of the war a few days earlier, there was no question of using the postal services, let alone making a phone call. From Verona, we were put on a plane to Naples. On the way, the American pilots were kind enough to fly low over Rome and then over the Bay of Naples, so that we could enjoy the beautiful scenery and incredible monuments. They were the heritage of mankind, and a foolish war waged by satanic psychopaths had nearly destroyed these wonders forever.

Once in Naples, the attitude of the Americans changed orthogonally. We were confined to our hotel rooms and not allowed to leave. GI's were assigned to guard us. We were not allowed to try to discuss anything: they pushed us back with brutality. Then we were taken to the prison camp of Aversa, not far from Naples. Back to the concentration camp world: confiscation of our meager personal belongings, confinement in a straw barrack, with a space of about ten square meters for three, filthy collective latrines, prohibition to write to our families... Fortunately, we were separated from the other German prisoners, that is to say the soldiers and the SS who had fought in Italy and had been captured as prisoners of war, and who considered us, the political prisoners, as traitors to the cause for which they had sacrificed themselves.

After four weeks in the Aversa camp, we realized that the Allies wanted to try some of us as war criminals. A group was taken away by plane: besides myself, there was General Halder, General Thomas, the industrialist Fritz Thyssen and some others. We were taken to France, to a small town near Versailles called Le Chesnay. There, in a large house that had been transformed into a prison, I found old acquaintances: the industrialist Ernst Heinkel, the famous aircraft manufacturer, some leaders of IG Farben, and Albert Speer, the architect who had become Hitler's Minister of Armaments. All of us were accused of crimes and we were waiting for the verdict: would we be judged by a court, and which one? A few more days and we were transferred by truck to Germany, to the castle of Kransberg, which had belonged to Hermann Göring and was now used as an internment camp for German personalities. The few weeks I spent there were not unpleasant: I had a single room thanks to the privilege of my old age, the food was excellent and the sanitary facilities were up to par. The interrogations were less pleasant: an English major was very correct, but I also had to deal with a small Jewish American who treated me worse than the ground.

In reality, all this was just an appetizer. My name, along with Albert Speer's, was placed on the list of criminals against humanity to be tried by the special court in Nuremberg. In mid-September 1945, Speer and I left the haven of Kransberg for the internment camp in Oberursel, where we were locked in real cages, completely open to the outside world and with no privacy. We were allowed ten minutes of walking per day, no more, and nothing to read or do all day. As for the food, it consisted of a vile, indigestible slop. Even worse than in Flossenbürg... A perfect antechamber to what awaited us in Nuremberg!

Colonel Andrus, who commanded the Nuremberg prison where we were locked up, once again in solitary confinement, made it perfectly clear to me when I arrived: as a former minister of Hitler, I was guilty. A criminal like me had nothing to expect from him. No special treatment, no request, no demand would be accepted. At least I have to pay tribute to this obtuse, primitive, low-brow American: he kept his word.

The section of the prison where I was locked up was reserved for serious criminals; the strictest isolation had to be observed between the accused. The regime was all the more severe because after the suicides in their cells of Robert Ley and Leonardo Conti, there was no question of the Allies losing another victim of their trial. Nevertheless, I could occasionally see with whom I was co-accused: Kaltenbrunner, Seiss-Inquart, Ribbentrop, Rudolf Hess, Field Marshals Keitel and Jodl, Hans Frank, Speer, but also Walther Funk, my successor as head of the Reichsbank, and that perverse sociopath Julius Streicher. As the weeks went by, I recognized a few others, including Hermann Göring, whom I met one day by chance in the bathhouse.

Most of the defendants were charged with four counts: participation in a conspiracy to start the war, participation in measures to prepare for the war, committing crimes during the war, and crimes against humanity. As far as I was concerned, according to the Allies, only the first two charges, conspiracy to start the war and preparation of the war, constituted my crime.

To be honest, at least 99% of the political leaders on this planet who once held governmental responsibilities could be accused of the same misdeeds.

What was my crime?

As Minister of Economics and President of a Central Bank, I had certainly financed the equipment effort of the Wehrmacht, the

German army. In doing so, I had simply carried out the classic government policy of providing one's country with a national defense. All governments do the same.

I therefore approached this accusation with a state of mind of perfect serenity.

I have never prepared for a war.

I never plotted to start a war.

I, Hjalmar Schacht, on the contrary, did everything I could to prevent it from happening.

Yes, in truth, what was my crime?

I had simply succeeded in restoring the economic power of my country, Germany, a great nation on which leonine and financially lethal conditions had been imposed at the Treaty of Versailles in 1919.

What was my crime?

For stabilizing the currency? Of having eliminated unemployment? After twenty years of hard work and constant sacrifice, I had achieved what no one else would have even dreamed of: I had been the author of the rebirth of a nation.

What was my crime?

For being more intelligent than others? To have been more industrious than others? To have been more imaginative than others? To have been more relentless than others? When I left the Reichsbank in 1939, the German currency was stable, Germany had full employment, my country had the most wonderful infrastructure network in Europe, roads, freeways, railroads, power stations, airfields, ports. German research was at the forefront of progress in all fields, aeronautics, naval industry, basic sciences, biology, medicine. Germany owed all this to me, Hjalmar Schacht! The ruined families of 1923, the rows of unemployed people of 1933 who haunted the soup kitchens, had been transformed into prosperous workers, who lived in comfortable cities and could travel by car on well-maintained roads to visit their relatives, to whom they had blithely telephoned from home to warn them of their arrival! Germany had twice as many telephones installed in homes as France or the UK! Thanks to me, Hjalmar Schacht!

What was my crime?

To have transformed a historical ruin into a historical economic success?

They could be jealous, those Frenchmen whom the German economic power had shaken like a straw. They could be envious, those English and Americans, who came to Germany to take advantage of the prosperity that I, Hjalmar Schacht, had restored with my ideas and my energy. I lost count of the number of large American or English companies that were lining up at my office at the Reichsbank or the Ministry of Economics to take advantage of the German revival and acquire stakes in our large companies: everything was good for them, automobiles, aeronautics, energy, chemicals, and even armaments! Yes, armaments! Germany's equipment effort would never have grown to such an extent or been so rapid without American capital. Many of the contracts I supervised were drawn up by American lawyers, including the firm of John Foster Dulles, Roosevelt's future Secretary of State. The same Roosevelt who asked me for advice to get out of the crisis! These contracts with our arms manufacturers benefited their big banks, the Chase or the National City Bank of New York. Today, what has become of those Americans who deferentially rushed to shake hands with Hjalmar Schacht and receive his anointment for their investments in armaments? My accusers! What immense hypocrisy!

What was my crime?

If there was a crime, half of the New York financial center, from Prescott Bush to the entire Morgan family, accompanied by a good *third of the American law firms and the entirety of the elegant bankers of the City of London, as well as the industrialists who constituted their clientele, had to sit next to me, Hjalmar Schacht, on the bench of infamy!*

For this crime, if there was a crime, was OUR crime!

The Russian generals present at the inaugural session of the Nuremberg Tribunal on October 18, 1945 were very strange jurists. This Nuremberg Tribunal is historic: the architects of the world war that has just ended are called to account to the whole of humanity. People and history must pass judgment on what has happened over the past five years.

In recognition of the superhuman sacrifices made by the Soviet Union in the fight against Hitler's Germany, the Allies decided that Russia would preside over the opening session of the special tribunal to try Nazi war criminals. General Iona Timofeyevich Nikichenko opened the proceedings.

What a nice personality, this Nikitchenko!

He is one of those rare historical communists who survived all the purges. A Bolshevik from the beginning, he joined the party in 1916, before the revolution, and survived Lenin, Trotsky, Stalin, Khrushchev, Brezhnev, and died in his bed in 1967, after the last Brezhnevian purges. Thanks to a boundless servility and a total lack of scruples, General Iona Nikichenko was a survivor. Not content with passing through the ages without ever knowing the Gulag, the Lubyanka, or even disgrace, he participated in the Stalinist purges as a judge in the trials of Grigory Zinoviev and Lev Kamenev, whom he sentenced to death with good humor for totally hypothetical reasons. He had them executed without appeal, the very next day after the sentence, before the families of these two historical friends of Lenin were exterminated in turn on the orders of Stalin, the red dictator.

Stalin was happy.

He appointed Nikichenko to lead the delegation of Soviet judges to the trial of Nazi criminals.

In fact, General Nikichenko was not the only historical communist with an extraordinary capacity for survival. Another specimen of the same species accompanied him to Nuremberg.

Roman Andreyevich Rudenko, for that is who he is, began his career in the opposite way to Nikichenko: the latter began by being a communist before becoming a magistrate, while Rudenko began by being a magistrate before joining the communist party. He did so late, in 1936. Then he tried to make up for lost time. He was a prosecutor at the trial of the Polish resistance, the famous "Trial of the Sixteen", in which Stalin, betraying all the guarantees he had given to the Allies on their honor, had the leaders of the Polish underground army who had rallied to him sentenced. Stalin did not like the Poles: between the Katyn massacres, about twenty-five thousand dead, and the million and a half Poles he deported during the invasion of the country, which he proceeded to do in 1939 in good understanding with Adolf Hitler, we can without exaggerating speak of animosity. Moreover, since the leader of the Polish underground army was only sentenced to ten years in prison during the "Trial of the Sixteen", Stalin had him executed by the NKVD in his cell; and then, for good measure, he also had most of the others executed. After all, why deprive himself? Rudenko had made a slight mistake with this too mild sentence of ten years in prison, and it could have cost him dearly. Fortunately, he made up for it after the war as commander of NKVD camp number seven: of the sixty thousand prisoners who passed through his hands, he managed to eliminate about fifteen thousand through malnutrition, epidemics, executions.

A satisfactory result.

Stalin was happy.

Rudenko had undoubtedly learned a lot about mass murder techniques during his stay at Nuremberg: he represented the prosecution there on behalf of the Soviet delegation. Like Nikichenko, the gentle humanist Rudenko also died in his bed in 1981; he was very old and had also gone through all the purges. Like Nikichenko, he had also helped to carry out the purges, for example during the trial of Stalin's damned soul, the sinister Lavrenti Beria, whose death he requested and obtained.

All in all, the Soviet delegation, which had the privilege of opening this trial that was to restore honor to the human race, looked good: its representatives were at least as unsympathetic and devoid of the slightest spark of humanity as the criminals they were to judge.

Fortunately, the Western bloc Allies had sent representatives of a different calibre: the French judge, Henri Donnedieu de Vabres, is a world-renowned jurist. The American judge, the elegant Francis Biddle, is the former U.S. Attorney General; a talented writer, he is married to a famous poet, Katherine Garrison Chapin. Finally, the Englishman Geoffrey Lawrence, hero of the First World War, is a rigorous, fair and just man; appointed peer of the realm after the trial, he will become 1st Baron Oaksey and will sit in the House of Lords but will continue to raise racehorses on his country estate. He could not help but feel a certain sympathy for Hjalmar Schacht, who had also become a follower of the simple, rural existence of the *gentleman farmer*.

The team that opened the debates of the Nuremberg trial in November 1945, a few days after the official opening session, was therefore rather disparate.

In reality, the Nuremberg trial was only one of the trials held in Germany at that time. Throughout the country, approximately five thousand Nazis charged with war crimes were prosecuted in the four zones of American, British, French and Soviet occupation. Eight hundred people were sentenced to death and a little less than five hundred were actually executed. However, the Nuremberg trial is the most prestigious, because it is above all the Nazi power and its high officials, such as Göring, Hess and Schacht, that are to be judged. Moreover, the place is highly symbolic: Nuremberg was the theater of the great masses of the Nazi gesture. The party congresses were held there in an atmosphere of pagan ceremony, with torches and flags, troops marching at a goose pace, and crowds of Nazi militants addressing the praetorian salute, arms raised high, to the all-powerful Führer Adolf Hitler. But this is not why Nuremberg was chosen: more prosaically, in a Germany often destroyed to the ground, the city of Nuremberg had infrastructures that were still more or less usable, i.e. a courthouse and a prison, conveniently linked by a tunnel, a large hotel for the delegations and journalists, and houses still standing that could be requisitioned to house the troops and the lawyers.

The list of war criminals to be tried at Nuremberg included twenty-four names. However, only twenty-one defendants were seated in the dock when the indictment was read: no one knew what had become of Martin Bormann, head of the Nazi party's chancellery and Hitler's right-hand man, who had disappeared when the Russians took Berlin. The very old Gustav Krupp, accused of exploiting captive labor in his factories and killing tens of thousands of these slaves, is completely doddering and will not appear. Finally, Robert Ley, the organizer of forced labor and mass slavery, committed suicide in his cell, as did an accused in another trial, Leonardo Conti, a doctor who organized appallingly cruel "experiments" on human guinea pigs in the concentration camps. These two suicides were the reason for the security measures surrounding the defendants: the lights were on day and night in their dungeons, and a GI was permanently assigned to watch over each of them, standing in front of the open window of their cell door.

The indictment took four hours to complete. The charges were crushing, inhuman; never before had so many acts of barbarity on so many innocent victims been attributed to so few men. The day after the reading of the charges, according to the Anglo-Saxon *common law* procedure used at Nuremberg, the defendants were called upon one after the other to declare whether they pleaded guilty or not guilty to the terrible acts for which they were accused.

One after the other, they stand up and ceremoniously say: *Nicht schuldig.*

Not guilty.

Not one of them, not even Hans Frank, who claims to be touched by the grace of God, acknowledges any responsibility for the horrors that were uttered during four hours.

Who are they, these so-called not guilty?

The twenty-one defendants can be grouped schematically into three subsets.

First of all, there are the high dignitaries of the government: Hermann Göring and Rudolf Hess, both former dauphins of Hitler, Hjalmar Schacht, Franz von Papen, Joachim von Ribbentrop, former Minister of Foreign Affairs, Konstantin von Neurath, his predecessor, and Albert Speer, former Minister of Armaments.

The second group was made up of the military: Marshals Keitel and Jodl, responsible for the conduct of the land war, and Admirals Dönitz and Raeder, their counterparts for the Kriegsmarine.

The third group is composed of the executors, the accomplices, those who called for the mass extermination or who carried it out: Here we find the *gauleiter* of the regions conquered by the Nazis and who carried out mass deportations of Jews, communists, gypsies and homosexuals, such as Hans Frank in Poland, Arthur Seiss-Inquart in the Netherlands, Wilhelm Frick in Bohemia-Moravia, Baldur von Schirach, former leader of the Hitler Youth and *gauleiter* in Vienna Alfred Rosenberg, former Minister for the Eastern Territories, and the disturbing Ernst Kaltenbrunner, a giant with a scarred face, successor to Reinhard Heydrich as Himmler's deputy and, as such, head of the SS and head of the concentration camps. Also included in this third subset are the psychopathic Julius Streicher, a compulsive and pathological anti-Semite, Fritz Sauckel, the organizer of forced labor in Germany where he deported five million people, and more secondary characters such as Walther Funk, Schacht's successor at the Reichsbank, or Hans Fritzsche, the radio announcer for the propaganda of the little doctor Goebbels.

If the magistrates have a disparate physiognomy, with a clear demarcation between the balanced jurists who make up the Allied delegations and the sinister Stalinist apparatchiks on the Soviet side, the defendants present an even stranger aspect: Rudolf Hess, looking lost, hardly seems to understand what he is doing there. This is probably the case: Hess is subject to bouts of amnesia, lapses of concentration and moments of apathy that make one doubt his sanity. Ribbentrop only sleeps when he is full of sleeping pills and is agitated by nervous tics. Hans Frank, the executioner of Sobibor and Treblinka, is taken over by a mystical madness: here he is from now on confessed in devotion, he who declared a few years earlier that all the trees in Poland would not be enough to hang all the Jews he wanted to exterminate. Julius Streicher soliloquized his anti-Semitic incantations, looking with a twisted eye at those who approached him and accusing them of being Israelites. Finally, to everyone's surprise, one of the most presentable was Hermann Göring. At the time of his capture, Hitler's self-appointed successor was a sickly obese person, his features distorted by alcohol and drug abuse, a morphine addict in the final stages of addiction. The Americans put him through a detoxification program. He came out slimmed down, fresh, free of his addictions, and more combative than ever. Göring found all his intellectual vivacity and the man made the show, bringing with humor or derision the contradiction to his accusers. Such is Hermann Göring: despite the terrifying accusations of mass murder and crimes against humanity, he cannot help but act like a star and even clown.

As for Hjalmar Schacht, he was not discouraged. Irritation is written all over his face. What is his crime? Yes, what is his crime, he who wanted to prevent the war, he who plotted against Hitler, he who knew his prisons and concentration camps? What is his crime? He looks at the court with a pinched look. Among the defendants, he is one of the only ones who hardly uses the headphones that translate the words of the court members: Schacht speaks fluent French and English. So he only uses the device for Russian. The glare he gives to the magistrates who accuse him is even more pronounced than that of the other defendants, who are forced to concentrate on listening to the devices.

The key moment of the trial took place a few days after the opening of the proceedings, at the end of November: in the main courtroom, a film was shown. It was a silent montage of reports made by cameramen and war correspondents, when the Nazi concentration camp world saw its gates open to the world.

It's awe-inspiring.

The long litany of human beings reduced to skeletons, the endless procession of children without hair or teeth due to malnutrition, the obscene spectacle of these mountains of martyred bodies piled up to unbelievable heights, the vision of these mass graves, of these gas chambers, of these crematoria... To imagine that this infernal organization was set up by these men, present in the dock, to wipe other men off the face of the earth and the memory of humanity, freezes the blood of the audience.

A nightmare.

Even Göring, during the projection, seems to shrivel up on the bench. Schacht is one of the only ones to hold his head high; the effect of the eternal hard collar shirts, no doubt. But he is affected, like the others, by the abominable spectacle. Some of the defendants had already seen excerpts of these images a few days before the screening. This is how Anglo-Saxon procedure works: the evidence must be known to the defense before it is presented in court. But all the defendants, for technical reasons, had not been able to attend this preliminary projection. For those who discover the absolute horror created by the Nazi regime, it is a shock. Worse than a shock: a trauma. Hans Frank, the terrible *gauleiter* of Poland, the creator of Majdanek and Sobibor, breaks down in tears. Rudolf Hess, who seemed to have a conscience that day, repeated: *Unmöglich* ("impossible"). Hans Fritzsche, the jovial announcer of Radio-Berlin, the voice of Goebbels for radio propaganda ("This is Hans Fritzsche!" he would cheerfully launch at the beginning of each broadcast), is devastated: he wants to change his defense and plead guilty. His lawyer talked him out of it.

The screening is all the more dramatically theatrical because the courtroom is plunged into darkness. Only the screen is lit on one side, where the appalling images of men, women and children crushed with unspeakable cruelty and a total absence of compassion, and on the other side the defendants, who remain lit by spotlights. The scene is striking of the executioners facing their victims and trying to keep the impassivity on their faces that seems to them to be in order.

But there is no goodwill to be had in the face of such horror.

There is only one choice: deny, always deny, deny against the evidence. This is what they all did. Göring, Kaltenbrunner, Rosenberg, Seiss-Inquart and the others, whose responsibility for the genocide of the Jewish population was not even debatable, all pleaded the same way: the culprits were Adolf Hitler, Heinrich Himmler, Reinhard Heydrich, Martin Bormann and Joseph Goebbels. These were the people who had organized the Holocaust. Convenient: they are all dead! As for the accused, they knew nothing...

In total, the Nuremberg debates lasted almost a year.

The interminable sequence of exchanges between the prosecution and the defense was sometimes broken by moments of great tension or grand guignol.

Great tension, when the Katyn massacres are mentioned, where twenty-five thousand Poles, officers, civil servants, students, in short, the elite of a nation, were mercilessly exterminated. The Germans blamed the Russians, but neither the prosecutor Roudenko nor the judge Nikitchenko would let them speak. They called to the stand the members of the Soviet commission of inquiry that had concluded that the Germans were responsible, and refused to hear the contrary testimony. But this was unacceptable to the jurists who made up the allied delegation. Several weeks of negotiations followed between Geoffrey Lawrence, Francis Biddle, Henri Donnedieu de Vabres on the one hand, and the Soviets on the other. A compromise was finally reached: the defense could produce three witnesses, and the Soviet prosecution as many. Roudenko, the man of the "Trial of the Sixteen" who knew perfectly well what to expect from the massacre of the unfortunate Poles by the NKVD, could triumph: the question of responsibility for Katyn would not be decided. Moreover, in the final decision of the Nuremberg Tribunal, Katyn was not even mentioned. Not very glorious for the Allies; in fact, President Roosevelt himself was ashamed of the Katyn affair. He had asked his ambassador to Bulgaria, George Earle, to investigate the massacre. Earle did a remarkable job of investigation, concluding that the Soviets were responsible. He asked the president for permission to publish his report. Roosevelt refused and immediately transferred George Earle to the Samoan Islands. It was important not to get angry with Stalin...

But the great tension sometimes gave way to the grand guignol: the Soviets brought to court *Feldmarschall* Friedrich von Paulus, the defeated of the battle of Stalingrad, whom they had captured and whom they had properly "turned" in favor of the Communist camp. Paulus accused Göring, Keitel and Jodl of having planned a war of conquest in the East as part of the Barbarossa plan, with the corollary project of exterminating the Russian prisoners of war who would be captured along the way. Göring exploded with fury, Keitel and Jodl inveighed against their former comrade, accusing him in turn of having launched calls for desertion that created all the more German victims... The session had to be suspended under the yells of the soldiers who exchanged insults.

By the time the charges against Hjalmar Schacht were to be examined, the trial had been underway for several months and it was March 1946. The proceedings took a much more serious, even monotonous turn. Schacht, as always, had a strategy. He called in a remarkable defender, Dr. Rudolf Dix, former president of the Berlin Bar Association. Together they drew up a defense plan. Hjalmar Schacht is an economist, a financier? So we have to be technical, meticulously technical, overly technical, in order to put the judges to sleep: talk about what Schacht did, rather than why he did it, and above all avoid mentioning for whom he did it. Talk about economic success, English capital, American banks, rather than the arms industry. And talk about Schacht's attempts to prevent war: the 1938 plot against Hitler. Unfortunately, there are hardly any survivors left to testify to this. But to their surprise, they find Hans Gisevius, the last of the conspirators, who comes to testify on Schacht's behalf. The American prosecutor Jackson, who is leading the charge against the financier, gradually gets caught in the latter's net, to the great fury of the Soviet magistrates. But when dealing with an outstanding negotiator such as Hjalmar Schacht, the game is difficult to win...

In the summer of 1946, the time came for the indictments and the pleadings. The French assistant prosecutor Charles Dubost, a great resistance fighter, who made the case against Hjalmar Schacht, was as precise as a surgeon:

"This evil man, who knew how to gather around him all the financial and industrial powers of the pangermanisantes to lead them to Hitler, who helped Hitler to take power, who inspired confidence in Nazi Germany by his presence, who knew how to provide Germany with the most powerful war machine of the time by his financial artifices, who did this to enable the party-state apparatus to conquer space, this man was one of the main responsible for the criminal activity of the party-state apparatus. His financial intelligence was that of the Nazi state, his participation in the state's crime is unequivocal. It is crucial. His guilt, his responsibility is complete."

In a few sentences, all of Schacht's work for Hitler is analyzed like a dissection. Dubost, in the name of France, calls for the death penalty against Hjalmar Schacht.

The verdict of the Nuremberg trial gave rise to numerous negotiations between the Allies and the Soviets. One of the disputes between the victors of the war concerned the nature of the death penalty to be applied to those condemned to death. Donnadieu de Vabres argued in favor of death by shooting. But the Soviets were inflexible: these wretches did not deserve a soldier's death. They should be hanged.

The Soviets win the decision.

The verdict was announced on October 1, in two parts: in the morning, the guilt of the accused with regard to the four charges was established. In the afternoon, the sentence is pronounced.

Hermann Göring, Joachim von Ribbentrop, Wilhelm Keitel, Alfred Jodl, Hans Frank, Ernst Kaltenbrunner, Arthur Seiss-Inquart, Alfred Rosenberg, Fritz Sauckel, Julius Streicher, Wilhelm Frick and, in absentia, Martin Bormann were sentenced to death by hanging.

Franz von Papen and Hans Fritzsche were acquitted.

The others were sentenced to various terms of imprisonment, including life for Rudolf Hess, Erich Raeder and Walther Funk.

And Hjalmar Schacht?

His case is one of the main controversies among the four judges. General Nikitchenko demands death. Geoffrey Lawrence wants acquittal. Donnedieu de Vabres wanted five years in prison and the American Biddle wanted life imprisonment. Finally, the court having already pronounced many death verdicts, Lawrence, the *gentleman farmer,* won the case: Biddle and Donnedieu de Vabres rallied to his opinion. Schacht was acquitted. But Judge Nikitchenko has one requirement: the verdict must specify that the acquittal is pronounced despite his formal opposition.

So it was done.

The acquittal of Hjalmar Schacht came as a huge surprise to the audience: defendants, lawyers, journalists, and prosecutors were all surprised by such leniency for the man to whom Hitler owed his power. Only one person showed any trace of emotion: Hjalmar Schacht. He was certain of the outcome; he had scientifically calculated the probabilities of getting away with it and meticulously worked out how to go about it.

Schacht was all the happier because, thanks to the Nuremberg Tribunal, he was finally able to see his little girls again. He feared that Constance, whom he had not seen since she was two and a half years old, had forgotten him; for Cordula, who was only 15 months old at the time of the separation, this was a certainty. Indeed, her eldest daughter had only confused memories of this father, in whose presence she was put in a strange room where she was separated from the old man by a grid. But the smile of this dignified hard-collared gentleman was gentle, and his eyes hidden behind his glasses seemed full of affection. Nevertheless, the little girl, held by her mother Manci's hand, did not want to go near the gate. When the end of the visit arrived, Constance could not stand it any longer: she walked up to the prisoner and proudly said to him, from the top of her 4 years, "You, I like you!"

Hjalmar Schacht, the great rational and unfeeling financier, cannot hold back a tear.

The convicts had four days to appeal for clemency to the Control Commission for Germany, a body set up by the Allies. Kaltenbrunner, Göring, Frank and Streicher refused to submit an appeal.

Useless, according to them.

Nevertheless, the lawyers for Göring, Frank and Streicher tried to lodge an appeal without informing their clients.

They were wrong and the condemned were right, for all appeals were rejected, including those of Keitel and Jodl who demanded death by shooting rather than by hanging.

In the former gymnasium of the courthouse, a gallows was erected. It was built by a specialist of the genre: the experienced Johann Reichhart, the Nazi executioner of the Plötzensee prison, author of three thousand one hundred and sixty-five executions in his career, with the axe, the guillotine or by hanging. Reichhart, among his titles of reference, was the executioner responsible for the execution of most of the condemned of the Valkyrie conspiracy.

Hitler's Ministry of Justice generally imposed "high and short" hangings, i.e. the condemned person was strangled by the rope under his own weight. For the sake of humanity, the Allies imposed the "long" hanging at Nuremberg: the condemned man, with the rope around his neck, fell from a certain height, breaking his cervical vertebrae and causing instant death. Johann Reichhart, after having built the gallows, shared his knowledge of death with Sergeant John C. Woods, the American army executioner, who was to officiate for the condemned at Nuremberg. It is said that he gave him very pertinent advice. The expertise he had acquired while executing opponents of Nazism was to be used for those who had ordered these executions: a singular paradox of the executioner's profession...

On October 16, in the night, the sentence must be carried out.

A little before midnight, a commotion shakes the prison of Nuremberg. A rumor swells. From their cells, the prisoners hear men running in the corridors, calling out to each other, shouting. Gates open, close, footsteps rush by, apparently in the direction of a cell in the section for those convicted of crimes against humanity.

The prisoners on death row are waiting for the execution that was announced to them earlier. They do not sleep; they are on the lookout.

What are these sounds?

What's going on?

Several minutes pass. The noises continue in the corridor.

Then the cell door is unlocked. Is it time to go to the gallows?

A man they don't know comes to talk to them in turn.

I must tell you that one of you is dead," said the stranger. Hermann Göring committed suicide. Cyanide. Get ready, the execution is in a moment.

The man leaves.

We close the door.

The silence returns.

Until...

That night, Sergeant John C. Woods executed, in one hour and forty-three minutes, the ten remaining death row inmates of the Nuremberg prison. All of them presented themselves to the gallows with dignity.

Except for one.

Julius Streicher, the pathological anti-Semitic madman, could not leave quietly. When he was picked up in his cell, he was in long johns and a body suit. He refused to get dressed. Okay, fine, he'll die dressed like that. They take him by the arm; he refuses to walk. He had to be dragged to the gallows. As the GIs tried to restrain him, he spat in their faces and shouted, "The Bolsheviks will hang you!" He had to be carried up to the platform of the gallows. Streicher yells again, "Purim, 1946!" a bizarre reference to a Jewish holiday. Finally, Sergeant John C. Woods manages to put the rope around his neck.

It is said that exasperated by Streicher's behavior, Sergeant Woods applied the "high and short" death to him, in other words strangulation by his own weight, much longer and more painful than the "long" hanging by fall that breaks the neck, which would be practically painless.

No one has been able to prove it.

Rumor had it that Sergeant Woods was relieved of his duties as an executioner in the U.S. Army shortly thereafter. He returned to civilian life and continued his career as an executioner in the service of his country's justice. But the executioner's career is not without risks: in 1950, while on a mission in the Marshall Islands and trying to repair an electric chair, he electrocuted himself and died, in a way self-executed!

Strange end for an executioner!

In his career, John C. Woods will have executed three hundred and fifty-eight people, a score nine times lower than his German colleague Johann Reichhart.

Not so bad though.

Hjalmar Schacht, acquitted by the Nuremberg Tribunal, is not done with justice. His acquittal caused an uproar in Germany. From all corners of the country, the last-minute resistance fighters demanded that he be brought before the denazification courts. These special courts, which operated until the early 1950s, tried about five thousand Nazi party dignitaries or assimilated and sentenced some of them to prison terms, often quite light.

When he was released from Nuremberg prison, Hjalmar Schacht tried to escape the action of these courts. He wanted to reach the British occupation zone, but did not succeed, and in the end, like so many others, he was caught up in the vengeance of those who had done little during the war and who wanted to redeem themselves once peace had been restored by their unhealthy activism. It is often the case that the despicable cowardice of hard times is replaced by an indomitable courage when security returns. In France, these people generally took revenge on women. They even went so far as to shear them. What brave heroes...

Schacht spent a few more months in various prisons, was sentenced for the first time to eight years of hard labor, and was finally acquitted on appeal.

In the meantime, he published a book with a rather curious title: *Abrechnung mit Hitler*, literally, *Règlement de comptes avec Hitler*, translated into French as *Seul contre Hitler*. With a certain amount of bad faith, he exposes his fight against the Führer, saying in passing a lot of bad things about the conspirators with whom he had associated, whom he accused of amateurism, even incompetence, and justifying very exaggeratedly the honorability of his conduct during the war as well as his lack of any responsibility in the accession of the Nazis to power.

In reality, this book, which could appear very hypocritical, is quite courageous. Indeed, despite the commonly held view, it was not so easy, just after the war, to assert oneself in Germany as an enemy of the Hitler regime, and even more so as a conspirator. In a Germany beset by all kinds of difficulties, those who had distinguished themselves by their plots against the old established regime were often regarded as traitors by the order-loving population. Thus, a man as remarkable and respectable as Baron Rudolf Christof von

Gersdorff, because he had plotted against Hitler, was turned down by the military when he wished to be reinstated in the Bundeswehr, the army of the Federal Republic of Germany, after the war, on the grounds that he had attempted to betray his chief command by trying to assassinate Hitler.

Schacht's approach, which in this book clearly asserted himself as an opponent of Nazi power, must therefore be examined in the light of this very particular state of mind. Far from being a proof of cowardice and opportunism, his work, although overly laudatory of himself, shows a certain courage.

In any case, once acquitted by the denazification courts, Hjalmar Schacht finally saw the end of his judicial ordeal.

At the beginning of the 1950s, he was free of all charges and was able to resume his normal life in Germany.

He is 74 years old.

Life begins.

CHAPTER 11. THE PHOENIX

In 1951, I was finally finished with the various types of tribunals, the Nuremberg Criminal Court, the denazification chambers, and all kinds of hateful civil servants who wanted to compensate for their frustrations by indulging in unbearable harassment of a former leader of the Third Reich.

I was ruined: by a miracle of geopolitics, my property in Gühlen was now in the German Democratic Republic, and thus in the communist zone. What was left of it after the fighting that had taken place during the invasion of Germany by the Russian armies had been seized and was now state property, subject to collective use.

It was the home of our past, of the happy days, of the war years spent in the countryside. It was also the scene of my arrest and exile to the concentration camps. Now it had to be forgotten.

Before the war, I also owned three small houses and an apartment in Berlin; everything had been destroyed in the bombing raids that had almost razed the German capital to the ground. In addition, to further accentuate my impecuniosity, the successive trials had exhausted my last resources; I was even heavily indebted to the lawyers who had defended me before the so-called courts of justice that had called me to account.

I had to find a way to support my family and myself. The books I had written provided me with an honorable royalty, but not enough to rebuild my former existence.

The ordeals of those terrible years would certainly have broken someone else: since July 1944, I had spent fifty-one months in prison or in an extermination camp, including two full years in isolation. I had been prosecuted like a criminal by the world and German courts. Seven times I had heard indictments that demanded either my head or long years of criminal imprisonment, so that at my age, finding freedom before the grave would have seemed like a dream.

However, the free man that I was, at 74 years old, had not lost his energy. Providing for my family was my concern at the time, and it was out of the question for me not to find a solution: I had two little girls whose education was still to be provided. For several months, I dithered between several options. Then came the light: fortunately, my reputation as the providential man of troubled economies had not been tarnished by the humiliating trials in which I had been dragged through the mud. I was known around the world as the financier who had beaten runaway inflation, the negotiator who had avoided paying off a debt that was leading to ruin, and the economist whose miraculous ideas had ended unemployment in his country. Indonesia called on me, then Egypt, then Iran, and others. They sought my advice to help them on the road to development.

These countries all welcomed me as a head of state.

Each of them defended their difference from the two great post-war blocs, the Western bloc on the one hand, and the Communist bloc on the other, not wanting to align themselves with either of them. They were therefore happy to receive answers to their structural problems from me. At least they had the assurance that the advice given by Hjalmar Schacht was not oriented in the interest of the adviser.

So I wasn't unemployed for very long.

However, the few months of idleness during which I had remained unemployed had further nourished my reflection on the economic and social scourge of unemployment.

In terms of unemployment, there is a threshold. This threshold is different in each country. Its level is conditioned by many parameters: government social assistance, the solidarity that exists in families, the more or less affirmed traditions of sharing, etc. Thus, this threshold can be very high in traditional countries with a strong family base and a Christian tradition: social and family ties then take over, up to a certain point, from the ties and resources provided by work. The threshold is significantly lower in more modern societies, whose development has been built on massive immigration attracted by the promise of jobs and a better life. In any case, it is important for governments to know what this threshold is, because when unemployment rises above this level, social ties begin to weaken, solidarity tends to be exhausted, and flight to all kinds of extremism is quick to increase.

Fighting unemployment then becomes the top priority. As I have often said, in terms of timing, nothing else should matter.

When the threshold for unemployment is reached, we must act, act quickly and act strongly. There is no point in delaying, in making excuses about economic difficulties, the global situation, or whatever. There is no point in implementing, as I have often deplored, repressive policies against the unemployed, who are made to feel guilty and even punished because they cannot find a job. If there are no jobs, it is illusory to encourage the unemployed to find work: there are none, that's all. You might as well be looking for the Grail: it doesn't exist. Under these conditions, stigmatizing the unemployed because they are unable to find a job that does not exist is heresy, even mental torture. This attitude, which is common among incompetent governments that are unable to create jobs, only increases the level of frustration among the population.

This was one of my advices to the Egyptian president, the Indonesian president or the Prime Minister of Iran: ask yourself the question of the threshold of resistance to unemployment. When your country approaches that threshold, act without delay and without regard for economic parameters such as the balance of public finances or the amount of debt your state has. These considerations become secondary. In terms of timing, that notion that is so essential in economics, you will have plenty of time to deal with the balance of accounts later on. Especially since, by reducing unemployment, you will naturally improve those financial parameters, such as the government deficit or the level of its debt, which worry you so much and which your partners and opponents monitor so closely.

If you act differently, you will encourage what you do not want at any price: instability, the rise of extremes, social disorder, or even worse: revolution, war, chaos. You will then have missed everything: you will not have reduced unemployment, you will not have improved the balance of your accounts, and you will have disappeared, carried away by the wind of history and revolt.

This was only one of the pieces of advice I gave to governments that came to me. It was always listened to when I was dealing with intelligent ears.

In addition to that, I also implemented programs of action to achieve development goals that we determined with the governments, or set up financial management frameworks, or renegotiated oil contracts with the major Western companies. And I have to say that, in general, the governments I assisted and I were successful.

Three years went by as we traveled the world. Wherever we travelled, my wife and I were welcomed with great respect. The Hitler years were well and truly forgotten; the governments that called on Hjalmar Schacht paid tribute to the economist.

However, as far as I was concerned, I felt that this role of international consultant could not be an end in itself. Even though I was called to the four corners of the earth to work with governments, my two little girls, Constance and Cordula, who had been deprived of their father for so long when he was imprisoned, could hardly stand my long absences. The youngest was just over 10 years old, and her older sister was 12: an age when the presence of a father is indispensable for building a balanced personality. Moreover, my sweet wife Manci, whom I always took on trips with me, also wished to lead a more peaceful life.

In 1953, I was 76 years old. Still a young age. I was in the fullness of life and felt full of life, will and plans.

I felt it was time to think about my future.

I had to find a stable situation.

So I decided to found a bank.

Indonesia, Egypt, Iran, Syria, India, Philippines, independent Algeria after 1963, and finally Peru.

In the 1950s and 1960s, Dr. Hjalmar Schacht was the go-to man for developing countries facing economic difficulties. Whether it was a matter of implementing structural measures, financial reforms or renegotiating contracts with large oil or industrial companies, Dr. Schacht was ready to help.

Until the age of 90, with his eternal dark suit, his hard collar shirts and his round steel-rimmed glasses, Schacht travels the world. He showed an uncompromising ethic in the political and economic choices he advocated; concerned with the successful development of these young nations, and not with pandering to the interests of one or the other, he put his science, experience and genius at the service of the non-aligned countries. Western governments did not always look kindly on this former collaborator of Hitler's coming to bring contradiction to lands they considered to belong to their sphere of influence. But Schacht did not care; when the representatives of the great colonial countries, France, the United Kingdom, or the United States protested to him to defend the establishment of their large companies in lands that they traditionally influenced, Dr. Schacht dismissed them with a few contemptuous phrases, accompanied by a haughty look.

He is right, he knows it and he lets it be known.

For Hjalmar Schacht, economic development was a factor of world stability; on the contrary, maintaining the newly independent countries in an economic system limited to the exploitation of raw materials for the sole benefit of the West could only stir up resentment in these young nations against the former colonizers, such as France or the United Kingdom, or against those who wanted to take their place in another form, such as the United States.

Economic development is about stability.

Underdevelopment and exploitation mean chaos, war and terrorism.

So, to take one example among others, when faced with a choice between the interests of British Petroleum or Standard Oil and those of the young Iranian population, Schacht had no qualms about sacrificing the oil companies. And there was no point in trying to intimidate the old financier: Schacht had lived through the hell of the concentration camps, the anguish of the conspiracies, the accusations of crimes against humanity and the pleas to have the death penalty imposed on him. So, intimidation, at his age and for a man like him... he is not a client!

Schacht moves forward, inexorably, along the path he has set.

In 1953, Hjalmar Schacht also decided to go back into business. He was 76 years old when he opened the windows of the Deutsche Aussenhandelsbank Schacht & Co in Düsseldorf, which specialized in international trade finance. His reputation in global financial circles is well established and his name is trusted. In finance, trust is the key to success. The Schacht & Co bank will therefore be successful; how could it not be?

Herr Doktor Schacht is not abandoning assistance to developing countries. But this was not entirely without risk. In 1954, he returned from a trip to Asia. Tired, he did not check the route of his flight from Calcutta to Rome. In fact, he had to change planes at the last moment and was guided in a hurry to the boarding of his replacement flight.

As the plane flies over the Persian Gulf, the pilot announces the planned stopover:

"Ladies and gentlemen passengers, this is your captain speaking. We will soon be landing at Lydda Airport, Israel."

Schacht feels a cold sweat running down his back. Israel? But that's impossible! His flight had to stop in Cairo, where he often works, and where he has many friends and powerful connections, like President Naguib! *Gottverdammt!* It's true that he changed planes! He didn't check where the stopover was. But Israel!... The Hebrew state had just come out of the war with Egypt, which Schacht advised very regularly; the armistice dated from 1949 and the military situation was still tense, often to the point of breaking down. Moreover, in Germany, the Jewish community was still very hostile to Schacht, whose acquittal at Nuremberg and then before the denazification chambers was still not admitted. Landing in Israel... it is lost! The Israelis are not going to lose such a great opportunity to seize, without any effort, a high dignitary of the Third Reich, and to judge him. Again the prison, again the confinement...

The plane lands on the runway of Lydda. The passengers disembark for the stopover. Schacht does not move.

- Sir?" asks a hostess. You should come down. We will stay here for three hours.

- Miss, I am quite tired. May I stay in my seat?

- No, this is impossible. The plane must disembark all its passengers. Please, follow me," says the stewardess, pointing to the exit of the aircraft.

- Exceptionally, miss, I would like to be able to rest here. I am really very tired. Think of my great age! insists the old financier.

- Sir, we will arrange for a seat for you to rest, but inside the terminal. You must disembark! Please, sir!

It was impossible not to comply. Hjalmar Schacht got out of the plane and walked slowly to the terminal. The crowd in the small building is not very large. Schacht tries to keep a low profile. He takes a seat on the buffet terrace in a secluded corner and orders a refreshment.

- Mr. President?

Schacht is the one who didn't hear.

- Mr. President? Are you President Schacht? The President of the Reichsbank? asks the waiter with a big smile.

- Uh... yes... it was... a long time ago... he answers.

- Mr. President!" the boy bursts out laughing. I served you in 1935, in Frankfurt! Ah, those were the good times! Business was good! Glad to have seen you again! Have a good trip, Mr. President!

The waiter walks away. Hjalmar Schacht is a little relieved. But then a Jewish lady and her husband approach and start staring at him unkindly. Schacht recognized them! He had dealt with them in an agricultural committee, if his memories are correct...

- Mr. President? Do you remember us? asks the lady.

- Of course... the committee? How are you?" asks Schacht with a smile.

- What are you doing in Israel?" the lady abruptly asks without answering.

- Just a stopover. I'm on my way to Rome. What about you?

- We leave for Chile. We settle down there. Business is bad here. Goodbye to you...

The couple moves away.

Catastrophe!" thought Schacht. In a few minutes, the whole terminal will know that Hitler's banker is sitting at the buffet, sipping soda water. With the Israeli organization he knows to be so effective, it won't be fifteen minutes before the Prime Minister's office is notified and orders are given to arrest him. No, definitely, what a bummer! He has no chance of escaping imprisonment. Moreover, the German government, preoccupied as it is with restoring cordial relations with the Jewish state, will not lift a finger in his favor!

The minutes tick by, slowly, very slowly. Schacht watches the clock with one eye and the other eye, dreading the arrival of the police to arrest him.

An hour passes. Then an hour and a half. Then two.

A call.

"Passengers for Rome please report to the boarding bridge! Departure in thirty minutes!"

Schacht gets up and with a vigorous step heads for the exit door. Once inside the plane, he breathes a sigh of relief.

The plane rolls onto the runway and then flies off. Hjalmar Schacht, Hitler's banker, is saved.

David Ben Gurion, the Israeli Prime Minister, was informed too late of Schacht's presence on Hebrew soil. If he had known in time, he would have had the old man arrested immediately.

But the Jewish state does not always have the same leniency, nor the same bad luck with former Nazis. What happened to some of these hierarchs of the Third Reich?

Wilhelm Stuckart left his office early on this day, November 15, 1953. After several weeks of rain in the Hanover area, the weather had finally returned to normal: a beautiful autumn day that made Wilhelm Stuckart want to escape to the countryside for an impromptu walk.

Wilhelm Stuckart would not be going home that night. On a perfectly paved road, with perfect visibility, a perfectly maintained car and a perfectly experienced driver, an accident occurred.

Wilhelm Stuckart died on the spot.

A perfect accident.

Or a perfect crime?

Stuckart was a former Nazi; he was co-editor of the Nuremberg laws on the segregation of the Jews and represented the Ministry of the Interior at the Wannsee conference that formalized the "final solution of the Jewish question. He had raised a few objections: according to him, in certain cases, a compulsory sterilization of certain populations would have been preferable to direct extermination, and would also have been easier to organize. But he did not insist. The Führer had ordered the Final Solution, so the destruction of the Jews of Europe was the only option. The despicable Stuckart had signed the conclusions of the Wannsee Conference and endorsed the policy of extermination. After the war, he was sentenced to a light punishment and released in 1949. A sentence that was far too insignificant for this faithful high official of the Jewish extermination...

It is said that on the evening of Stuckart's fatal accident, four Mossad officers were leaving the industrial area of Hanover in a truck coming from Stockholm to deliver a load of paper to Geneva.

It is said that they were present earlier in the day at the scene of the accident...

It is said that Mossad has a long memory.

But so many things are said...

Years later, in May 1960, a Mossad commando kidnapped in Buenos Aires a modest foreman of a Mercedes-Benz car factory named Ricardo Klement. Apparently, the Mossad had a mission to take good care of this unknown man. Klement was held for a few days in a villa in the Argentine capital, and then put on an El Al plane bound for Tel Aviv. Ricardo Klement's real name was Adolf Eichmann. If Hitler inspired the Final Solution of the Jewish problem, if Himmler and Heydrich were the architects who imagined the death camps, the mass executions and the industrialization of the process of attrition of the Jews, Adolf Eichmann was the tireless organizer. He built the camps, devised solutions for transporting the victims to their place of execution, devised the means to take life on a large scale, and developed the devices to deal with the problem of rendering the bodies in acceptable sanitary conditions. Eichmann, that small and zealous civil servant, wanted to be the supreme administrator of the Holocaust. His defense, during his trial in Tel Aviv for crimes against humanity, was to affirm that he had followed orders.

He was sentenced to death and hanged.

Yes, Mossad has a long memory...

However, in spite of the Mossad, like Hjalmar Schacht, some Nazi hierarchs had successful careers after the war and died very peacefully in their beds.

A great career, but no peaceful death for *Untersturmführer* Hanns Martin Schleyer: this SS, who became the great leader of the German employers, did not die in his bed, but was murdered by the German terrorists of the Red Army Faction (Rote Armee Fraktion - RAF), otherwise known as "Baader's gang", in 1977.

Another brilliant career was that of Hans Globke, a faithful collaborator of Wilhelm Stuckart, the participant in the Wannsee conference mentioned above. Globke was one of the authors of the Nuremberg laws and decrees on the segregation of the Jews. He became State Secretary of the Federal Republic of Germany and was one of the closest collaborators of German Chancellor Konrad Adenauer. Baron Rudolf Christof von Gersdorff, this hero of the anti-Nazi struggle, owed it to Globke's animosity to be forbidden all his life to rejoin the army, pursued as he was by the contempt of this Nazi who did not like those he considered traitors to Hitler.

During his terms as Chancellor of the Federal Republic of Germany, Konrad Adenauer, to whom Globke was indebted for his rise to the top of government politics, supported the Nazi whom he had made his advisor. However, Adenauer was forced to resign because of another Nazi, *Obersturmführer* Heinz Felfe. A former spy of the Third Reich, Heinz Felfe continued his career after the war in the secret services of the Federal Republic of Germany. In 1950, he was recruited by the KGB. A few years later, as he rose in rank, the double agent Heinz Felfe was put in charge of the fight against the KGB in Germany; just like Kim Philby in the United Kingdom, this traitor in the service of the Soviet Union now controls the fight against Soviet espionage! Heinz Felfe was unmasked in 1960, ten years after his betrayal in favor of the communist bloc; the scandal pushed Adenauer to retire from political life. It is true that employing a former SS man as a master spy to fight the KGB, and then finding out that he was actually spying for the Soviets, was rather messy.

As for the anti-Semitic Nazi Globke, when after his retirement he wished to retire to Switzerland, the Swiss authorities, who during the years of the Great Reich had been much less fussy, declared him persona non grata and forbade him to settle in their territory.

Even better than Globke, in the pantheon of Nazis with a magnificent career, is Kurt Georg Kiesinger. This ambitious character was an extremely active member of the Nazi party from 1933 onwards. A close associate of Joachim von Ribbentrop, he was in charge of Nazi propaganda outside of Germany, hence his flattering nickname of "Goebbels from abroad". Imprisoned after the defeat of Germany in 1945, he was released in 1948. He entered politics a few years later, and in 1966 became the powerful chancellor of the Federal Republic of Germany, a position he held until 1969. A Nazi at the head of West Germany! Just that! As a small consolation, he was humiliated by Beate Klarsfeld, the Nazi hunter, who publicly slapped him by calling him: "*Nazi! Resign!*" Needless to say, he will do nothing of it.

Further up the ladder of world leaders, here is a young lieutenant, member of the Nazi party, husband of a convinced militant of the Nazi cause, and intelligence officer of the Wehrmacht during the repressive campaign led by the Nazi army in the Balkans between

1943 and 1945. During this murderous punitive expedition, numerous atrocities against civilians were committed by the German forces. This lieutenant, a convinced Nazi, who took an active part in these horrors under the conditions one can imagine, later became Secretary General of the United Nations between 1972 and 1981 and President of the Austrian Republic between 1986 and 1992; his name was Kurt Waldheim.

So there was a bright future for the former Nazis.

Hjalmar Schacht also tried to enter politics in the 1950s, but his name was too sulphurous to be welcomed into a party. He gave up his responsibilities in Germany and devoted his time to his bank and to developing countries. Among the countries he helped most often was Egypt. First in the service of King Farouk, then from 1952 until 1953 for the Egypt of President Naguib, and finally from 1953 for the Egypt of President Nasser.

He was not the only German to come and retrain in Egypt.

The SS *Obersturmbannführer* Otto Skorzeny was a hero of the Third Reich. A commando officer capable of the most perilous dares, he was notably the leader of the parachute detachment that freed Mussolini from the mountain prison where the opponents who had overthrown him were keeping him prisoner; this was in September 1943. With Otto Ernst Remer, he also participated in the failure of the Valkyrie conspiracy on July 23, 1944, by leading the assault against the insurgents entrenched in the Bendlerblock, the Wehrmacht headquarters in Berlin.

After the war, he fled to Spain and founded the Odessa organization, which helped former Nazis escape from Europe to South America. At the instigation of General Gehlen, a former Wehrmacht officer and post-war founder of the German secret service, Skorzeny went to Egypt in 1953 as a military advisor. He took with him several high-ranking officers of Nazi Germany: a panzer division general, an elite SS officer, a former head of Hitler's personal guard, and others.

At the time, Egypt was in a state of latent war with Israel, the young nation where the survivors of the Shoah had found refuge. Egypt, like the other Arab nations, did not want to accept the creation of this Jewish state where, at last, after two thousand years of wandering, the Semitic diaspora would have a refuge of its own. A first conflict had taken place between Egypt and Israel in 1948-1949, and a second one would soon break out in 1956: the Suez War.

It is interesting to note that the Nazis, through Otto Skorzeny in the military field and Hjalmar Schacht in the economic field, saw their unreasoned hatred of the Jews continue in a certain way in the service of a country, Egypt, whose declared will at the time was to wipe Israel and the Holocaust survivors who had found a home there off the map.

But Hjalmar Schacht, as far as he was concerned, certainly did not pursue this goal. He had shown that he was not a man of war. War means chaos, ruin, the end of development. The economist that he was did not want that. On the contrary, harmonious economic development for the benefit of all was his credo until the end of his life.

In fact, in his old age, Hjalmar Schacht revealed more and more of his humanity, which he had concealed for so long; it was time.

One day, he is in Indonesia and bathes in a pool after a long day of work. It is very hot and humid; many bathers surround him and young Indonesians come to greet this dignified European old man, with his somewhat severe air, but who seems amused to be there, surrounded by the youth of the country. We start to discuss economy, currency, development... Themes that Schacht is fond of. Then one of the bathers says to him:

- You know, three years ago, talking to you here would have been impossible!

- Is that so? Schacht is surprised. And why?

- The pool was off limits to us, the colored people. It was reserved for white people, or the leaders of the country. Now we can come and talk to you.

Hjalmar Schacht's face lights up with a huge smile. He was overjoyed. Things are moving in the direction he wants.

Hjalmar Schacht's work for the development of emerging countries is considerable: reforming the administration of the young Indonesian state, setting up the Central Bank of Syria, renegotiating Iranian oil contracts, building the Algerian financial system, developing growth in Peru, organizing the state in Egypt... Who can claim to have done as much for the economic development of countries newly freed from the yoke of colonization as Hjalmar Schacht, Hitler's financier, the devil's banker, the man who had made the Second World War possible?

While traveling to distant destinations where governments were eagerly awaiting him, Schacht frequently had to stop en route, as non-stop intercontinental flights did not yet exist. He stopped several times in Calcutta, India, on his way to Indonesia. During his visits, he discussed economic problems with the country's ministers. He was received by Pandit Nehru, the liberator of India, and by his daughter, the young Indira, who was so charming and intelligent that she left Hjalmar Schacht with the memory of an exceptional personality. Yet Schacht was not one to be easily impressed. But this young girl was to have a destiny that elevated her to the firmament of the great leaders of history: she was the future Indira Gandhi, who governed India, the largest democracy on the planet, for some fifteen years before her assassination by a soldier of his personal guard. No doubt she took advantage of the great financier's visits to her father's house to better understand how a country's economy worked, and learned from Hitler's banker how to guide nations on the path to development and prosperity.

In this respect, if we take stock of the great world leaders who were once enriched by Schacht's advice to guide their economic policy, we realize to what extent this man, by giving his wise counsel to their leaders, influenced the destiny of hundreds and hundreds of millions of other men: before the war, in addition to Adolf Hitler, he advised Franklin Delano Roosevelt on how to get out of the great crisis that had started in 1929. Then after the war, he was the advisor of Naguib and Nasser the Egyptians, of Mossadegh the Iranian, of Soekarno the Indonesian, of Ben Bella and Boumédiène the Algerians, of the generals in power in Syria, of the Peruvian president Terry, historical leader of the country, and finally of Nehru the Indian and his daughter Indira Gandhi. Excuse the little...

Hjalmar Schacht's place in the global economic geopolitics of the second half of the 20th century makes him the equal of the greatest heads of state.

And to think that for his crucial role in the Hitler tragedy, he should have been hanged in Nuremberg!

The years passed. The children grew up. The grandchildren too. Great-grandchildren were born. Revolutions were declared. Crises shook the world: the cold war, decolonization, the Cuban missiles, the Prague revolt, the coups in South America and Africa...

Life simply flows; and one day it approaches its end.

At the beginning of June 1970, Hjalmar Schacht's inexhaustible energy left him. He admitted it cheerfully on his birthday in January, surrounded by his children, grandchildren and a few babies of the new generation: at 93, he is now an old man. Sweet Manci, when she heard the confession of weakness of this unshakeable husband, this rock whose life she has shared for almost thirty years, went out into the service to stifle a sob.

The spring air coming down from the Bavarian mountains is mild, but the nights are still cool; they are filled with the scent of flowers blooming in the countryside. It is a pleasure to breathe, as it was in the spring of 1944, when the great financier was freed from the Nazi concentration hell. That was in the Tyrol, not far from here.

The vast Munich apartment is quiet; sweet Manci tries to keep it quiet, which is not easy with the grandchildren and great-grandchildren of the great man. But Grandpa is very tired, so the little ones walk slowly when they pass his room, in the middle of the long hallway that is so much fun for wild rides.

Hjalmar Schacht will die.

His eternal dark suits are stored in his closet. His hard-collared shirts, carefully ironed, have remained in his drawers for several weeks. His round, steel-rimmed glasses lie on the bedside table.

On June 3, 1970, the famous financier, the greatest economist of the 20th century, the man who saved Germany from ruin three times, fell asleep serenely, with a sense of duty accomplished.

The devil's banker hands over his soul to God.

Let's hope for him that it is so.

CHAPTER 12. INHERITANCE

Hjalmar Schacht wrote a lot throughout his life: twenty-six books in which he expressed his ideas about the economy or in which he recounted his experiences or his life. Apart from a few rare pages, Schacht reveals very little of his personal feelings. Most of his writings are devoted to his work as an economist in the service of Germany or to his ideas on politics and government.

This complex man has two very different aspects.

On the one hand, as an economist and financier, Schacht always managed to find miraculous solutions to the gigantic challenges he was faced with. Whether it was a question of overcoming galloping inflation, putting an end to the payment of reparations, reviving the German economic machine, fighting unemployment, restoring his country's balance of trade, or leading developing countries on the path to growth, he never failed. This is a unique case in history.

On the other hand, as a man, he was often wrong. He was wrong about Adolf Hitler, whom he believed he could control and manipulate. He was wrong about Hermann Göring, who happily betrayed him. He was mistaken about Nazism, a doctrine that in no way corresponded to his deepest thoughts. Finally, he was mistaken about himself: in wanting too much to appear as the insensitive and rational man in charge of the German economy, preoccupied only by his sense of duty, he forgot that he undoubtedly preferred, deep down in his repressed "self", the simple life of a family man in the countryside. His internal exile in Gühlen and his years of imprisonment had a revelatory effect on him: Schacht realized that there were other values that deserved to be given a share of his time.

The end of his life, after his liberation, was more balanced than the first part, where his whole being was preoccupied with economic success, political power and his place in history.

Schacht II thus appears more human than Schacht I.

However, there are several lessons to be learned from Schacht II and Schacht I.

The first is determination. This man who survived so many trials, who overturned so many mountains and took on so many challenges, had an incredible determination, on a par with that of a de Gaulle or a Churchill, who were also exemplary in terms of inflexible will. Determination is the sine qua non of success in any field.

The second is foresight. Schacht is not a theoretician. Despite the abundance of his books, he did not write masterpieces, he did not compete with Keynes in the field of economics or Jacques Rueff in the field of money, nor with any of the authors who are references on the university benches. No, he did much better: he acted. Confronted with insoluble problems, he examined, analyzed, imagined, and then implemented his solutions, without changing course, without dogmatism, with the strength that comes from a conviction supported by deep reflection. And he won.

The third is the general interest. Schacht was a business genius. He could have built up a colossal global fortune. But no, this kind of superficiality was not worthy of him. He was not self-interested:

a dark suit, a hard collared shirt, a pair of steel-rimmed glasses... there was no taste in Schacht for wealth, ostentation, the imbecilic and selfish greed that characterizes the modern capitalist system. Schacht was concerned with development for all, which he believed guaranteed social stability.

Determination, foresight and general interest: this is the legacy of Hjalmar Schacht.

Of course, some will point to other, much less presentable legacies. Self-esteem, pride, the certainty of always being right, arrogance, superiority complex, ego bloated with contentment... of course, there is also that... but please, can we not forget these shortcomings in favor of the inventory of virtues that the great Hjalmar Schacht has transmitted to us?

Today, at the beginning of the 21st century, when a global crisis of unprecedented violence is raging, one can only dream of what Schacht would do if he were still in this world, populated mostly by leaders who are vain and concerned above all with themselves. In France, their cardinal concern is only to win the next election at all costs in order to safeguard their privileges, without even attempting to change the course of the country. In Germany, the objective is to maintain the advantages acquired over the other European countries, even if it means crushing them economically and crushing their hopes of recovery. In the United Kingdom and the United States, the unanimously shared doctrine is to pursue a resolutely individualistic course, without taking into account the disruptions that this causes, and while apologizing very civilly but without really believing it: "*So sorry!*

What would Schacht do?

In 1933, Hjalmar Schacht revived the German economy by creating from scratch a new kind of quasi-currency, the MEFO bonds, and by engaging the country in an unprecedented effort of equipment, industrialization and, unfortunately, also armament. He established strict control over the use of the resources he generated and the distribution of the profits he made. In this way, he overcame unemployment in less than five years: starting from a situation of seven million unemployed, that is about one and a half million unemployed people back to work each year. Who can compare to him?

No one, alas. And especially not today's political leaders, while economic difficulties are piling up and shaking a continent like Europe to its foundations, whose leaders seem definitely powerless to revive prosperity.

What could Hjalmar Schacht imagine, if he were still present, smoking a cigar in a damp, dark office where mops are drying?

Have the presidents, chancellors, and ministers who occupy the gilded palaces of republics and kingdoms retained nothing of his legacy, especially those among them who record disappointment after disappointment in the conduct of their nations' economic policies?

As described in this book, Schacht's greatest successes were achieved in three areas: monetary stabilization, debt renegotiation, and the fight against unemployment. Let us analyze the present situation with regard to these issues, all of which are marked today in many countries by deep imbalances that seem impossible to restore; and let us examine the solutions that Schacht imagined.

In monetary terms, the situation we are in is obviously not the same as it was in Schacht's time, in 1923. He was faced with record hyperinflation, whereas today we are in the opposite situation: deflation threatens our Western economies. However, the causes of the evil, in some respects, are identical: indeed, the hyperinflation was partly - but only partly - due to speculators, to financiers who played the dollar against the mark and contributed to pushing their own country into the inflationary spiral from which these profiteers in elegant suits skilfully drew the fruits. The Western economies, on the other hand, were plunged by the bankruptcy of Lehman Brothers in 2008, which triggered a financial crisis in the global banking system, followed by a sovereign debt crisis, all of which culminated in an economic crisis that spread to the entire planet. In both cases, 1923 and 2008, the financial system bears a heavy responsibility: in Schacht's time, because of its resolutely selfish and greedy attitude, which led to a worsening of hyperin-flationary tensions; and in 2008, because of its inability to control its own risks, and in particular the recklessness of its traders, who multiplied operations whose consequences they themselves did not understand.

The measures decided then by Hjalmar Schacht and those decided by modern leaders are diametrically opposed: in 1923, Schacht decided to cut off the taps of financing to speculators, even if it meant causing their ruin, and this overnight. There is nothing comparable in 2008: the political and economic authorities who had to deal with the financial crisis, as best they could, took the exact opposite position. For them, the banks had to be saved at all costs. As a result, very costly rescue plans were implemented by national authorities in Ireland, Greece, Germany and elsewhere, to the extent that during the period 2008-2012, in Europe, 10% of the continent's GDP was absorbed by the rescue of banks. The balance sheets of the Central Banks are now full of dubious assets bought from the financiers, who were previously guilty of having triggered the crisis, in order to allow them to survive. It is the community that now bears the associated risks.

Thus, in this first aspect of monetary policy, Hjalmar Schacht has remained an isolated example in history. Modern economic authorities have not sought to draw inspiration from him: the devil's banker, a former banker himself, did not hesitate to sacrifice his fellow men. For their part, today's leaders, who are often also former bankers or come from the same waters, do not spare the people's money to save their fellow believers.

However, what Schacht had done had worked rather well...

The second great economic achievement of the devil's banker was the renegotiation of German debt. Hjalmar Schacht's credo in this matter has always remained the same: if debt is a problem, it is not only a problem for the debtor, but also for the creditor. The creditor must therefore participate in the solution of the problem. For Schacht, this principle was expressed in a very concrete way by an unequivocal attitude: if he lived, Germany would not pay! Period! And he organized things accordingly, during the debt renegotiations with the Dawes Commission, and then with the Young Commission. To be honest, he behaved with open dishonesty, for while he appeared to be openly discussing how to restructure the payments, his deepest intention was not to pay a single pfennig! And he succeeded!

Today, many countries are weighed down by the weight of their debt, which hinders any economic recovery. In this situation, the attitude of the political and economic authorities has consisted rather in imposing on the impecunious debtors, i.e. countries such as Ireland, Portugal, Spain and above all Greece, austerity measures of terrible intensity, in order to free up budgetary margins to ensure the repayment of this debt. For those who are not yet completely on the brink, such as France and Italy, the prospect is nevertheless that they will have to pay one day. As a result, the states concerned are projecting themselves into the situation of having to pay, i.e., they are implementing recessionary austerity policies, even as their unemployment rates tend to explode. In this way, the ranks of the unemployed continue to grow and no significant economic recovery is possible. It is true that, very exceptionally, sacrifices have been imposed on certain creditors when the situation was too compromised; this was the case for Greece's private creditors. But in the end, the remedy has always consisted of maintaining the debt ball and chain, in a barely lightened form, and demanding in exchange an austerity that condemns without appeal any hope of a return to prosperity, at least in the short and medium term. As for hopes of a better life in the long term, we are entering the realm of faith, because in the long term, as Keynes said, everyone will be dead. Perhaps even before: in Greece, at the end of 2014, the country has experienced five consecutive years of recession; the unemployment rate has reached 26% of the working population, it exceeds 60% among those under 25, and the suicide rate has risen by 40%. Yet there is no question of the masters of European economic policy deviating from the trajectory: if the country survives this purge, it will be cured, it seems. But will it survive?

Hjalmar Schacht was viscerally attached to the demand for quick results. "Where is the promised recovery?" he would ask our modern leaders. Schacht had done everything to free Germany from the burden of debt, including abusing goodwill, like that of Dawes and Young. This was the only permissible method in his mind. It has not occurred to our modern leaders to follow his example in solving the debt problem. Probably not by simply refusing to pay, as Schacht had skilfully done, but by "monetizing" this debt, or part of it, with the central banks, at the rate of their interventions with the banks, i.e. about zero per cent.

Because what Schacht had achieved had worked rather well...

The third brilliant success of the devil's banker was the fight against unemployment. Hjalmar Schacht, starting from a situation of more or less seven million unemployed when he returned to the helm of the German economy in 1933, managed to put them all back to work in less than five years. He had absolutely no financial means to do this. Schacht therefore invented the subtle mechanism of pre-financing through MEFO bonds, which would make it possible to finance productive investments and infrastructure, and also to equip the Wehrmacht with the most modern weapons. In short, he achieved a real miracle in the reduction of unemployment.

Don't worry, there is no question of asking our modern leaders to walk on water or to multiply bread rolls. Each to his own; miracles are reserved for exceptional beings and very few of today's leaders can claim this quality. However, it is obvious that in most countries in crisis of underemployment, the recipes used by the authorities to try to reverse the unemployment curves never deviate from the old outdated methods they have abused since the beginning of the development of unemployment in the 1970s: subsidized jobs, tax aids, training courses endlessly renewed, in short expedients whose beneficial effect is extinguished as quickly as the flame of a candle when the storm blows. It is true that sometimes higher ambitions emerge. But they generally come up against the wall of financing: in our countries with exsanguinated public budgets, no one dares to use "Schachtian" methods to create money, and consequently jobs.

Yet, following Schacht's example, it would be possible to set up structured financing in an original way: not with MEFO bonds, although the idea deserves to be explored again, but, for example, by means of a large investment fund constructed with ingenuity. Its so-called *equity* part, in other words the fraction that would absorb the first possible losses, would be subscribed by the governments, followed by semi-public investors, such as the caisses de dépôts et de consignation, which would hold the junior debt, and finally private investors, who would subscribe to tranches of increasing seniority, mezzanine and senior.

A hermetic lecture, typical of the abstruse and indigestible jargon of financiers, isn't it?

The author apologizes for using such unliterary verbiage, but this galimatias means, in essence and in republican French, that states would take more risks than private investors who would be very protected; quite simply. Such a mechanism would create a tremendous leverage effect and generate considerable resources. Framed "à la Schacht", these resources would be likely to be mobilized in the form of productive investments that create wealth and sustainable jobs. And of course, there is no question of diverting them to put plasters on wooden legs, such as the subsidization of unproductive jobs, destined to disappear once the funding envelope is exhausted. A method in keeping with the spirit of Schacht as a providential man, in short.

For he, the devil's banker, had succeeded magnificently in overcoming unemployment...

In the end, who is right? Who is wrong? Was it Schacht? Is it today's leaders? Judging by their respective achievements, the conclusion is easy, and old Schacht wins unanimously; but the judgment is probably a little too cursory, because things are complex and difficult. This is, in any case, what those who govern today, and who are no longer able to influence the course of their nations' economic life, tirelessly explain.

Should we blame them?

There is no obvious answer to this question, but if asked, Schacht would undoubtedly point out, with his characteristic arrogance and haughty tone, that there are two kinds of men: those who have results, and those who have explanations.

He, Hjalmar Schacht, had results.

Why did Hjalmar Schacht succeed where others fail today? Who was this man? A liberal? A socialist? A Keynesian? He defined himself as a supporter of capitalism, although he admitted that he did not like this terminology. He prefers to use the term capitalism-individualism. The definition is not bad, especially if one wanted to define the nature of capitalism as we know it in our modern societies, but it does not really fit Schacht.

Although he defended the law of the free and open market in his writings, Schacht was in fact a staunch interventionist.

In 1923, and throughout the monetary crisis, he either opened or closed the floodgates of credit, depending on his assessment of the currency and inflation situation. In 1933, as head of the Reichsbank, he directly financed major state projects, something that Western central banks today totally prohibit. To restore Germany's balance of trade, he introduced strict import controls through the administration of the Ministry of Economics; in other words, he imposed protectionist measures, which are now prohibited in the world of the global economy. Finally, he was a fan of the planned economy: *Neue Plan, Vierjahresplan,* that was the way he operated. None of this is the work of a liberal economist; on the contrary, a Soviet economist of the old cryptocommunist school would love such a method.

But Schacht is anything but a communist. At least, that is what he claims.

Hjalmar Schacht was essentially a rationalist. If the economy had to be financed to create jobs, he preferred to do it himself, at the head of the Reichsbank, rather than rely on the hypothetical collaboration of the banking system, whose perspective was resolutely selfish and individualistic, with its eyes fixed on the profit curve. Today's economic and monetary institutions think in the opposite direction: rather than intervening directly in the real economy, they prefer to deliver free money to the banks, in gigantically disproportionate quantities, and hope that the latter will use it to finance companies and that they will create jobs. So far, the results are not very tangible. Obviously, with such a poorly oiled set of gears, the present system cannot be as effective as Schacht's, who preferred to take matters into his own hands, with his loyal Reichsbank staff to support him. Direct intervention, hands-on: for Schacht, the great mechanic of the economy, this was the way to effectively repair a broken engine.

In the same way, today, countries with a dangerously unbalanced trade balance are forced to maintain open relations with the outside world, bound as they are by an inextricable set of treaties, agreements and norms, originating from the European authorities, the World Trade Organization or other regional sub-groups that structure the planet. For the dogmatic ayatollahs of free and open competition, it is better to make a country's companies die, even if it means creating unemployment, than to renounce the sacrosanct principles of non-intervention by the State and the free movement of goods and capital. It is by clinging to this blind neo-liberal doxa that the competition authorities are killing entire sectors of activity, some of which are subsidized by the State, but which nevertheless play a useful economic role.

In order to justify this toxic mindset, the economic decision-makers behind this doctrine invoke at every turn the Austrian economist Joseph Schumpeter, whom they have not read or understood, but from whom they have retained the notion of "creative destruction" to justify sacrificing companies and jobs in the name of free trade. They forget that the term "creative destruction" begins with "destruction", which gives it a somewhat disturbing tone. The battalions of unemployed people, for their part, see on a daily basis that it is much easier to destroy jobs than to create them.

For Schacht, this could not be tolerated: in his view, the protection of the internal market was necessary if useful activities were to be safeguarded. He therefore did not hesitate to limit the opening of the German market to the outside world and to take drastic measures to limit imports of goods and services. And he restored Germany's balance of trade, thus contributing to the country's general prosperity on the eve of the Second World War.

Schacht, with his characteristic good sense, would remind the advocates of universal free trade that the economists who inspire them, like Adam Smith, lived in the 18th century or earlier. They developed their beautiful theories of market efficiency by observing the economic conditions of a civilization where globalized trade did not exist, where the mobility of goods was hampered by modes of transport and where the instantaneous circulation of capital was impossible. In short, Hjalmar Schacht would explain with hauteur and condescension to contemporary economic decision-makers that applying to a globalized postmodern world the free-trade theories of eighteenth-century economists, whose only observable perspective was an economic environment close to that of prehistory, is nonsensical and can only lead to disaster.

Some of the countries he advised have learned their lesson: in 2014, India, inspired by the memory of Hjalmar Schacht, succeeded in bending the World Trade Organization to continue subsidizing its food production for the poor. The Torquemada of free trade, safe in their air-conditioned offices where they walk around in their elegant Armani suits, Hermès ties and luxury shoes, wanted to subject these basic food products to the ruthless iron law of open global competition, in defiance of the hollow stomachs of hundreds of millions of poor people who depend on these essential agricultural commodities for survival. The brave Indians have been allowed to remain in open violation of the terrifying inquisitorial rules of globalized international trade; a beautiful victory of reason against the absurd law of blind liberalism. Is the message of the devil's banker beginning to win over the minds of people?

Hjalmar Schacht is thus a paradoxical liberal. Some would say a schizophrenic liberal. Let's call him a rationalist; that's the only word for it. Unfortunately, the species is on the verge of extinction. Too bad for us.

So, to conclude, dear *Herr Doktor* Schacht, is your legacy so sulphurous that almost no one, in this modern age, thinks of using it anymore? What would your ghost advise us to do in order to get out of the crisis that strikes the world at the beginning of the 21st century?

Let's dream for a moment.

He would answer that: "There is today a war to prepare, but not a military war: it is a war even more dangerous, a planetary war against global warming and energy consumption, whose effects will be so devastating that they may make some countries bordering the great Pacific Ocean disappear, and that they could make whole areas of Africa or elsewhere uninhabitable."

Schacht would then launch a battle plan in his own way: "I will organize a formidable research and investment plan, financed by a temporary increase in state debt, a plan that will create jobs in pollution control, energy transition, positive energy buildings, devices to limit greenhouse gases and eliminate the particles that make the mild spring air unbreathable. We will pay off the debt needed to finance this war plan with the dividends of saving money on fossil fuels! Thanks to me, we will get it done!"

As Schacht remains Schacht, he would probably add, with the arrogance, the superiority complex and the bloated ego of contentment that were inseparable from his immense genius: "I give myself enough credit to believe that I will succeed in this enterprise! Anyway, there is no alternative! Failure is not an option!"

Adolf Hitler's banker would anticipate that such a plan would represent development for all, Western countries, countries in transition, poor countries.

Obviously, Hjalmar Schacht's dream can only be realized by Hjalmar Schacht. This is a pity, because the devil's banker is no longer there and has not been replaced.

But you have to dream a little.

Afterword 1932-2015, from Heinrich Brüning to François Hollande: In Search of Clairvoyance

How can one not be struck by the similarity of the economic and political situation in Germany in 1932, just before Adolf Hitler came to power, and the state in which some European countries, particularly France, find themselves in 2015?

In 1932, Germany was plunged into an unprecedented global economic crisis, which had begun a few years earlier in the United States. The country had more than six million unemployed. Germany was led by a chancellor whose popularity had plummeted to an all-time low; almost no one trusted him anymore, even in his own camp. He is a rather honest man, presenting himself as an economic specialist, but he has shown a profound lack of foresight in his diagnoses and economic choices. Indeed, while the country was embroiled in an extremely violent recession, the chancellor embarked on a relentlessly rigorous deflationary policy: the priority objective that he pursued under pressure from other European countries, and to which he sacrificed the well-being of his population, was the reduction of public deficits and the recovery of the state's accounts. Nicknamed the "Chancellor of Hunger" because of the pressure he put on the middle classes, he was driven out of office before the end of his term. The despair he had sown in the country led to an irrepressible rise in right-wing extremist parties, which would soon take power.

Let's take the risk of transposing the preceding paragraph to the French way, in a contemporary way.

In 2015, France is immersed in an unprecedented global economic crisis, which began a few years earlier in the United States. The country has more than three and a half million unemployed. France is led by a president whose popularity has plummeted to an all-time low; almost no one trusts him anymore, including in his own camp. A rather honest man, presenting himself as an economic specialist, he nevertheless shows a profound lack of foresight in his diagnoses and his economic choices. Indeed, while the country is embroiled in an extremely violent recession, the president is committed to a relentlessly rigorous deflationary policy: the priority objective he is pursuing, under pressure from the dominant country in Europe, Germany, and its European allies, and to which he is sacrificing the well-being of his population, is the reduction of public deficits and the recovery of the State's accounts. Nicknamed Pépère by the members of his cabinet because of his lack of authority, his hesitations are numerous and his reversals of opinion frequent, but he always returns to the same old recipes: pressuring the middle classes, who are already burdened with taxes, and avoiding the slightest substantive reform in order not to upset anyone. However, the despair he sowed in the country caused an irrepressible rise of the right-wing extremist party, which under his presidency became the first party in France.

The resemblance is striking, isn't it?

Fortunately, the end of French history is not yet written.

The end of German history is described in detail in this book. The fate of Heinrich Brüning is not mentioned: Brüning, who had decided in 1932 to dissolve Röhm's SA and the SS - yet another decision that was never followed by this decidedly weak man - was forced to flee Germany in 1934. He settled in the United States where he taught economics at Harvard. Let us hope that he learned from his serious mistakes in economic policy and passed on to his students better principles than those he implemented when he was in power. He died in Norwich, Vermont, in 1970.

Historical comparisons obviously have their limits, and we can bet that the disastrous fate of Europe at the end of the 1930s will not be that of Europe today.

However, the example of Brüning is rich in lessons.

First of all, Brüning was a weakling, which quickly discredited him in the eyes of the German population. However, this man was a weak man with two sides. On the one hand, he was dogmatic to the point of absurdity. Like a barnacle tied to the hull of a sinking ship, Brüning was incapable of breaking away from the strictest economic orthodoxy, to the point of leading his country into a recessionary abyss from which only the genius of Hjalmar Schacht could escape. On the other hand, with the extreme right-wing movements and in particular the Nazi party, he did not know how to react, and when he did, it was too late. Moreover, in his reactions, he showed himself, as usual, excessively timid, hesitating to firmly implement his own decisions, such as the forced dissolution of the SA and SS.

In France, the discredit that affects the President of the Republic is of another order: the gap between his exercise of the presidential function and the values that he imprudently proclaimed during the electoral campaign is indeed too obvious, in the eyes of the population as a whole and of his voters in particular. For example, his famous speech at Le Bourget, in which he stigmatized finance as his enemy, has been translated in reality by his unwavering support for the aforementioned finance: first by implementing a minimum of his project, however salutary, of separation of speculative activities of banks. Then, by intervening very awkwardly with American President Barack Obama to limit the sanctions incurred in the United States by a French bank guilty of violating an embargo in favor of a country, South Sudan, which the United States had blacklisted because of the mass murders committed by its army against ethnic minorities. Finally, he called in a wealthy investment banker to advise him, and later made him his Minister of the Economy. At no time did this electoral "animosity" against finance find an echo in the French president's policies. Yet it was finance that was responsible for the financial crisis of 2008.

The discrediting of the French president is also attributable to his promise not to mix public functions and private life. While he made this question a central criticism of his predecessor, whom he will beat in the second round of the presidential election, never since the late Felix Faure, who died at the Élysée in the arms of a semi-mondaine, has the president spread his vaudevillian private life so widely in the celebrity press of the station halls. Between the turpitudes of the *first girlfriend* interfering in a legislative election, to the repudiation in public of the ex-favorite by a sovereign whose many commentators will then say that the muflerie disputes with the goujaterie, and then the revenge of the spurned one by way of a best-selling book denouncing, on the part of a supposedly left-wing official, an unbearable contempt for the poor, the French president has fed the gravelly discussions of the dinners in town of the whole planet. As for the stories of the nightly scooter ride to an actress' bed and the croissants shared at breakfast... some have written that the dignity of the presidential office has reached the heights of ridicule in France at this time: President of the Republic, in the manner of a pimply schoolboy! They tell us that in Colombey-les-Deux-Églises, visitors have been hearing General de Gaulle turning over loudly in his grave with great regularity.

At least the dignified Heinrich Brüning, the austere Catholic bachelor with an uncompromising personal ethic, had not sunk so far into the irrationality that the exercise of power sometimes provokes in weak minds.

On the other hand, the German chancellor of the 1930s and the French president were similar on two points: their lack of economic foresight and their weakness in the face of external pressure.

To analyze the state of the economy objectively is certainly not an easy task, and one must be careful in this exercise. Brüning had, above all, lost his way on solutions, stubbornly sticking to his deflationary vision when the opposite was necessary, as Hjalmar Schacht would brilliantly demonstrate a few months after the resignation of the "Chancellor of Hunger. As for the French president, he also made a mistake in the observation: announcing as a certainty the reversal of the unemployment curve in 2013, when there was no sign of such optimism, and a cruel denial by the continuous increase in the battalions of unemployed will persist for many months, or congratulating himself in July 2014 on the shuddering growth finally returned, when a few days later INSEE will announce exactly the opposite, results in destroying any form of credibility. This is obviously all the more embarrassing when one has placed one's five-year term under the sign of economic recovery, as the French president has done: this blindness to the stigma of the crisis does not help to inspire confidence.

Credibility can also be acquired in another way, by showing character in the face of external pressure. Here again, Brüning and the French president were on an equal footing. Brüning was unable to resist the Allies who wanted to force Germany to respect certain clauses of the Young Plan, which restructured German debt and the repayment of war reparations. These payment clauses were clearly unbearable for the German economy, which was plunging into a downward spiral of recession. As for the French President, he is currently unable to counterbalance the injunctions of Mrs. Merkel's Germany, relayed by the European Commission, for whom the recovery of public finances is an absolute priority that must take precedence over all other considerations. For Mrs. Merkel, today's German chancellor, the dogma of balancing the state's accounts cannot be transgressed, even when the unemployment rate cheerfully exceeds 12%, as in France, and even when it is around 25%, a situation from which the populations of Spain or Greece are suffering. Brüning had an excuse for adhering to this dogma: the dramatic hyperinflation was less than a decade old. Hjalmar Schacht had succeeded in putting an end to this hyperinflation at the end of 1923, after three years of monetary madness, and all the Germans of 1932, including Brüning, remained traumatized by the memory of the ruin they had experienced during those painful years. Today, things are diametrically different: inflationary pressures are almost extinct, at least in the world of developed economies. However, no one is thinking of taking advantage of this historic opportunity to launch a vast investment plan capable of reviving the economic machine and thus ending or reducing unemployment; and especially not the French president, who is faithfully following German instructions.

For German policy, and consequently that of the European political, economic and monetary authorities, remains deeply marked by the spectre of the German hyperinflation of the 1920s, which they blame for the rise of Nazism and the ensuing world war, which caused the destruction of half of Europe.

But both the Germans and the Europeans are making two analytical mistakes.

The first mistake is historical: much more than the trauma of hyperinflation, it was the rise in unemployment that brought the Nazis to power in Germany between 1930 and 1933. In this respect, Hitler understood the situation perfectly: what did he ask Hjalmar Schacht when he appointed him president of the Reichsbank? To restore the balance of public finances? Not at all! On the contrary, he asked him to mobilize every conceivable means to get the last of the unemployed off the street. For Adolf Hitler, the end of unemployment was a factor of social stabilization, and thus of consolidation of his power. It is sad to say, and painful to write, but in this respect, that monster Adolf Hitler was right.

The second analytical error is economic. By imposing a deflationary policy on Europe, Mrs. Merkel is pursuing a precise goal. For her, the economic crisis is a crisis of public finances. Consequently, the imbalance in public finances must be eliminated as quickly as possible. Mrs. Merkel is supported in this by the financial markets, which welcome any new austerity effort, just as the same markets greedily buy the shares of large companies that announce massive layoff plans. Driven by this double German-European and market-financial pressure, the governments of the other European countries have no choice but to multiply their announcements of austerity, savings and austerity, with tens and tens of billions of cuts in social budgets, infrastructure investments and support for populations in difficulty. The confidence of international investors and of Mrs Merkel is at this price. General de Gaulle used to describe them as cabbages jumping on their stools shouting "Europe! Europe!"; today they are still jumping, but yelping "Austerity! Austerity!"

Are they at least right? Have the countries that have adopted these dramatic austerity plans redressed their public finances?

The answer to this question is unquestionably negative: none of the countries of the South, which have been pursuing this deflationary policy "à la Brüning" for the past four years, has seen its debt disappear during this period. On the contrary, the debt has continued to grow and the accounts of the states are still unbalanced. And during this time, activity has slowed down, bankruptcies have soared, and the number of unemployed has multiplied: in 2014, Europe has ten million more unemployed than in 2009.

But Mrs. Merkel, whose country benefits from a monetary advantage at the head of Europe, due to a particularly advantageous euro exchange rate for German exporters, continues her injunctions unperturbed. And the European Commission is faithfully following. And so do the French president and his government, which is chasing the unemployed and sacrificing family policy, despite the great success of French public policies, while at the same time making unbearable declarations of love to the population: "The government loves companies", "The government loves the poor", "The government loves families"; this is the government's slogan for every announcement of new austerity measures. At least we can think that the communication agency that invented this strange oxymoron has seen its budget explode: a fine invention, abused by the French president and his ministers, that consists in sermonizing curious speeches of affection while imposing harsher sacrifices on loved ones who do not ask for so much.

By dint of imposing deflationary policies, our modern Brünings end up winning their bet: the whole of Europe, including Germany, begins to sink into a deflationary spiral: lower investment, lower production, lower prices, lower wages and then lower consumption, which leads to lower investment, lower production... and the circle continues ad libitum. In short, a situation from which no one, as far as one is informed, has the slightest idea of how to get out.

Not everyone is Hjalmar Schacht.

On the contrary, adopting a policy of growth and job creation, as Schacht did so well, would naturally lead to a recovery of public finances. Of course, such a policy can only be undertaken at the cost of a temporary drift in the budget of the States; one country, Japan, has taken this path. Japan is the only country, for the moment, to have chosen the future and not a deflationary retreat. The others prefer to move, solidly grouped, towards deflation, like a flock of sheep fleeing an imaginary danger and tumbling together into an unfathomable and dismal precipice.

What an odd choice...

Meanwhile, in France, the National Front has become the leading party in France, winning many important municipalities in the last elections in 2014 and crushing the traditional parties of the right and left in the European elections. Two members of the Front National have even been elected to the Senate. They are following the path set out in Greece by the Golden Dawn party and its shaven-headed Nazis, in Austria by the nationalist and populist parties that governed Carinthia, in Belgium by the Vlaams Belang, and by many others.

Heinrich Brüning, during his time in the German chancellery, had missed just about everything.

The French president, until now, has more or less followed the same path in the recovery of the French economy and it is not sure that the fall in oil prices and the euro, two phenomena to which he is a total stranger, are enough to save him, even in appearance.

Let's hope that a new Hjalmar Schacht will one day show him how to change that...

The French president would thus avoid harsh judgments such as this one, made in 2006 about one of his predecessors by a politician who was running for the presidency of the Republic and achieved his goal in 2012: "...[he] will have finally done the country a service by the length of his mandate, by the repetition of his failures, by his way of acting, by this permanent defeatism, by this feeling of impunity, by this permanent disempowerment, by the incapacity that was his to take risks, to make his choices and to expose them to the country. In short, he will have given the image of a counter-presidency, as one would say a counter-indication[1] .

By the way, wasn't this politician, the author of these lines, the current tenant of the Élysée Palace? Now that he is installed in the president's chair, wouldn't he find it difficult, as he wrote about another, to take risks, to make choices and to expose them to the country? Hjalmar Schacht, in his *Memoirs,* said this: "I hate two kinds of men: those who shirk their duties and those who, after the fact, know everything better than everyone else. It's hard not to fall into one or the other; and sometimes even into one AND the other.

---

1. Opinion expressed about the president of the Republic Jacques Chirac by François Hollande in his book *Devoirs de vérité,* co-written with Edwy Plenel and published in 2006 by Stock.

Unlike Heinrich Brüning, may the French president find in the example of the devil's banker some ideas to make up for the time he has wasted in simply enduring the global crisis, while waiting for the next election and a hypothetical resumption of growth. The task is certainly immense, and probably even insurmountable. However, even insurmountable challenges are worth taking on for those with good intentions. Schacht was undoubtedly one of those unyielding souls, forged from indestructible stainless steel. And since he was also gifted with a prodigious analytical intelligence, success awaited him at the end of the road.

What was Hjalmar Schacht's recipe for dealing with the insurmountable economic challenges he faced with the success we know?

It is based on three principles. Identify what the priority is; devote all possible and impossible means to solve it; have a strategy for less than five years.

And to put the strategy to music, show determination, more determination, always determination!

Unbeatable!

This is the final lesson from beyond the grave of Hjalmar Schacht, the devil's banker, the man who succeeded in this essential field of economic policy, at the heart of the life and prosperity of peoples.

Something to think about...

BIBLIOGRAPHY

Works by Hjalmar Schacht:

Das Ende der Reparationen [*The End of* Reparations], Oldenburg, Gerhard Stalling Verlag, 1931. English translation (United States) by Lewis Gannet, *The End of Reparations*, New York, Jonathan Cape and Harrison Smith, 1931.

It is important for the world to think like a businessman! Drückerei der Reichsbank, Berlin, June 1935.

Abrechnung mit Hitler [Settling of accounts with Hitler], Hamburg, Rowohlt Verlag, 1948. French translation, *Seul contre Hitler*, Paris, Gallimard, 1950.

Mémoires d'un magicien, 2 volumes (*De Bismarck à Poincaré* ; *De Hitler au monde nouveau*), Paris, coll. "Toute la ville en parle", Amiot-Dumont, 1954.

Author's note: Chapters 1 to 11 of the book open with a first part in which Hjalmar Schacht speaks and evokes his life, his economic thinking or the people he met. This is by no means a duplication of his works, but the author's interpretation, as realistically as possible, of Hjalmar Schacht's state of mind as it is reflected in his writings or in the way he behaved and acted.

Other works:

Adenauer (Konrad), *Memoirs*, 4 volumes (1945-1953; 1953-1956; 1956-1963), Paris, Hachette, 1965-1969.

Beevor (Antony), *La Seconde Guerre mondiale*, Paris, coll. "Sciences humaines et Essais" Calmann-Lévy, 2012.

Brissaud (André), *Canaris. Le "petit amiral", prince de l'espionnage allemand. 1887-1945*, Paris, Librairie Académique Perrin, 1970.

Clavert (Frédéric), *Hjalmar Schacht, financier and diplomat (1930-1950)*, Peter Lang Verlagsgruppe, Bern, 2009

Gersdorff (Rudolf Christof, von) *Killing Hitler. Confession of a German anti-Nazi officer*, Paris, Tallandier, 2012.

Goldensohn (Leon), *Les Entretiens de Nuremberg*, Flammarion, 2005.

Kageneck (August, von), *La Guerre à l'Est*, Paris, coll. "Tempus", Perrin, 2002.

Kageneck (August, von), *Examen de conscience. Nous étions vaincus mais nous croyions innocents*, Paris, coll. "Tempus", Perrin, 2004.

Kersaudy (François), *Hitler*, Paris, coll. "Maîtres de guerre", Perrin, 2011.

Kersaudy (François), *Hermann Goering*, Perrin, 2009.

Kershaw (Ian), *Hitler*, 2 volumes (1889-1936 ; 1936-1945), Paris, Flammarion, 1999 and 2000.

Longerich (Peter), *Goebbels*, Paris, Héloïse d'Ormesson, 2013.

Moczarski (Kazimierz), *Entretiens avec le bourreau*, Paris, coll. "Folio histoire" (n° 192), Gallimard, 2011.

Schlabrendorff (Fabian, von), *Officiers contre Hitler*, Paris, Éditions Self, 1948.

Speer (Albert), *Au cœur du Troisième Reich*, Paris, Fayard, 1971, reissued in the "Grand Pluriel" series, Fayard/Pluriel, 2011.

Varaud (Jean-Marc), *Le Procès de Nuremberg. Le glaive dans la balance*, Paris, Librairie Académique, Perrin, 1993.

Wilmots (André), *Hjalmar Schacht (1877-1970). Grand argentier d'Hitler*, Brussels, Éditions Le Cri, 2001.

Table of Contents

www.ingramcontent.com/pod-product-compliance
Lightning Source LLC
La Vergne TN
LVHW010212060726
842525LV00014B/3285